Here's what reviewers are saying about this book . . .

". . . bound to stimulate thinking, and offers wise counsel for many parents who are struggling as their children move from dependence to independence. . . . It's long on the why's and the how to's of family living, and short on speechmaking and sermonizing."—MOUNT HERMON ASSOCIATION.

"Parents who are open-minded and sincerely willing to receive counsel on the relationships to their children will find this book stimulating, thought-provoking, at times irritating, but always interesting. Author Shedd's opinions cannot be too lightly brushed aside since he speaks from a background of his dealings with thousands of teenagers."—THE WESLEYAN ADVOCATE.

"Readers believe an author like Charlie Shedd. He is concise, witty, accurate. There is no gaudy splash of verbiage (rhymes with garbage). He makes his point and finished, stops. Shedd has another appeal. He likes his readers. He thinks they are intelligent. He gives enough to work on but the reader can do the rest. His time is in great demand by others. He knows his readers' time is valuable too. A reader appreciates this consideration. . . . He comes on strong as a fellow-parent-human being who has life clearly in focus."—WARNER ROBINS (Georgia) DAILY SUN.

"There's a reason for Charlie Shedd's books becoming best sellers. When he speaks you know there won't be any phoniness. And when he deals with life it is with joyful contagion that spreads like a disease. Reading this book has given me the bug to do better parenting. I like all the new ideas his family has tried and proved workable. . . . Excellent for church libraries."—PROVIDENT BOOK FINDER.

"Shedd is an honest writer. He does not claim to have all the answers. And he is highly effective. Frank, sometimes controversial, he turns new ground in your thinking."—ILLINOIS BAPTIST.

"Unique, both in its subject matter and in its unconventional, colloquial style."—PRESBYTERIAN JOURNAL.

"Excellent, easy reading . . . appeal for all—from teen-agers through golden-agers. Read it. You won't put it down!"—CHRISTIAN HOME AND SCHOOL.

"A rich mine of wisdom and inspiration for parents."—TOGETHER.

"A positive how-to for parents who would like ideas in helping their child become an independent mature adult. Dr. Shedd underscores the need for each person to be himself and guides parents toward that goal for their children. There are times when it all seems too easy, but just when you are saying to yourself, 'Ah, come on now, Charlie,' he verbally throws up his hands with other parents and admits there are no best answers in some situations; some things are just lived through (helpful knowledge for parent and child). . . . Excellent material for discussion between parents and teens around the dinner table."—HOUSTON CHRONICLE.

"Written without the use of mind-boggling psychological terms. It is a simple book with a lot of 'good horse sense' about parent-child relationships. . . . Its simple guidelines will be warmly welcomed. Church librarians would be well-advised to secure a volume."—AUGSBURG BOOK NEWSLETTER.

"A wealth of down-to-earth information for a better family life."—SIOUX FALLS ARGUS-LEADER.

"Shedd has a broad, practical, intuitive knowledge of human relationships, drawn from people rather than from books—from his own family, his parishioners, the psychiatrists on whose hospital board he served and the many teenagers he has counseled. Evangelical in tone, the thrust of the book is training a child for self-discipline and self-government, so that he can manage his own relationships to God and to man. Certainly this is a thrust that is needed in our day, when children, deprived of right ways to grow up, try so many wrong ways."—ETERNITY Magazine.

"A magnificent book—to give or to cherish!"—BAPTIST SUNDAY SCHOOL BOARD.

"The author is right with it when it comes to everyday modern problems. He never claims to be perfect as a parent (far from it), and he is able to turn psychologists' pet phrases like 'self-actualization' into English. It's not just parent-English, either. In most cases, it's the kind of book a kid could hand a parent without worrying that the parent would misinterpret and that the text would backfire. . . . The book gives parents not only insight but motivation to operate courageously with the newly acquired knowledge. There are also guidelines to help a parent determine the difference between permissiveness and the wholesome encouragement of self-government."—BOSTON PATRIOT-LEDGER.

"The book will be read with profit by all parents who are sincerely concerned about their children and are perplexed about the decision-making process."—CHRISTIAN STANDARD.

"Dr. Shedd makes a strong case for parents' responsibility in teaching children how to work. 'Who is the most unhappy person on the youth scene today?' the author asks. Answer: the full-time noncontributor. . . . The book resounds with positive good sense. But if such a book is heartening to parents, imagine what it can mean to their offspring!"—ARKANSAS BAPTIST NEWSMAGAZINE.

"A fresh, give-and-take look at the ingredients necessary for a full, rich family life . . . and what each member of the family must pitch into the pot. It is must reading for anyone who seeks that magic relationship between parent and child—true friendship."—PENTECOSTAL PUBLISHING HOUSE.

"Parents searching for ways out of ruts will find practical ideas for family devotions, family council, family fun-nights, and jobs and allowances. Buy and study Shedd's book as preventive maintenance if you have a child two or older. And keep the volume handy for when you feel like throwing up your hands for help. Or sitting up late with your spouse."—CHRISTIANITY TODAY.

YOU CAN BE A GREAT PARENT!

Other books by Charlie W. Shedd

The Exciting Church: Where People Really Pray
The Exciting Church: Where They Really Use the Bible
The Exciting Church: Where They Give Their Money Away
The Fat Is in Your Head
Is Your Family Turned On?
The Stork Is Dead
Letters to Karen
Letters to Philip

YOU CAN BE A GREAT PARENT!

charlie shedd

WORD BOOKS, Publisher
Waco, Texas

YOU CAN BE A GREAT PARENT!

Originally published as PROMISES TO PETER *by Charlie W. Shedd.*

ISBN 0-87680-861-5
Library of Congress Catalog Card Number: 76-128353

Printed in the United States of America

First Printing—August 1970
Second Printing—October 1970
Third Printing—June 1971
Fourth Printing—August 1972
Fifth Printing—February 1973
Sixth Printing—June 1974
First Paperback Printing—February 1976
Second Paperback Printing—May 1976
Third Paperback Printing—July 1976
Fourth Paperback Printing—September 1976
Fifth Paperback Printing—May 1977

Today's young give me high hope for a better tomorrow
From speaking often on the college scene
Rapping with the high schoolers
Reading their letters by the hundreds
I see good things coming on

Like Peter
Twenty-three now
And also like Margie, his wife
Individually
Together
They are some kind of beautiful

THIS BOOK IS FOR THEM

Prologue

How to Raise Your Children

This was the title of one of my finest efforts. Like all good speeches it had unity, order, movement. It electrified, edified, specified! It grabbed them quick and held them fast with humor, pathos, drama!

All over the midwest I gave it. They paid me a handsome fee and they were glad to get me. "This guy will wow you!" That's what they said, and the people came. With high hopes, they came for "How to Raise Your Children."

Then we had a child!

That sound you just heard was the great elocutionist falling flat on his face. My majestic speech (honest it *was* great) had been totalled. Those brilliant ideas had such a droll sound at 2:00 AM with the baby in full cry!

In my defense I want you to know this—I kept on trying. I changed my title to "Some Suggestions to Parents," and charged bravely on. Then we had two more children and I altered it again. This time it came out "Feeble Hints to Fellow Strugglers."

From there it was all downhill. The appeal was out of it. My drawing power moved to zero. (I forgot to tell you the honoraria went down with each revision.) But for another thing, I couldn't stand to hear me.

So today I seldom speak on parenthood. And whenever I do, after one or two old jokes you'd catch this uncertain sound. . . . "Anyone here got a few words of wisdom?"

But enough of this. What do *you* know for sure? Well, whatever it is, for God's sake pass it along.

That was not a slip from the writer's id nor a swear word for emphasis. If the Lord of history looks for a civilization on which He can build permanently; if the home *is* our number one shaper of human character; if these two things are true, then so is this—parenthood is all important!

How our children turn out may make the difference!

That puts us moms and dads right in the center of tomorrow's destiny, doesn't it?

As a father of five and lover of their beautiful mother, I've discovered a few things. In fact, the seven of us have learned a lot together. And some of the things we've learned are the subject of this book.

Charlie Shedd

Contents

The Original Promises to Peter *

This is for Peter Jay. He was born early this morning. (Preacher's sons *should* be born on Sunday morning.) Although he is less than twelve hours old, he is a very unusual child. Dr. Arrendell said so. He has delivered some three thousand babies and every one of them was favored to have him there. Such a wise doctor should know a bright child when he sees one. So, I would have a word with my new son.

It's a great life, Peter, and I'm glad you were born into it. We wanted you very much. For the past nine months we have been talking about you. Actually, we have been thinking of you for years.

Your mother and I fell in love when we were very young. I remember the picnic when we sat in the park, talked about our babies, and named you. So you have been in our dreams a long time. For five years after we were married there were no babies. Then Philip came. He did us so much good the Lord looked down one day and said, "They need another baby." And here we are now, with three more because the first one did us so much good.

Philip, Karen, and Paul have taught me much. We've learned a lot together. Like "How to" and "How not to." Therefore, there are some things I want to promise you.

---

* Peter, our fourth child, was born at the ebb flow of my beautiful theories. But before my idealism went under completely, I did make one last effort. On the day of his birth I made him a compact. "Promises to Peter" was first published as a magazine article (*Household Magazine,* August 1953, Cappers Publications, Inc.). From there it traveled many ways and far. One day my editor said, "Since Peter is grown, why don't we republish your original pledge?" The rest of *You Can Be a Great Parent!* is the record of how we've done.

First, I pledge that I will remember always it takes a lot of love to make good children.

You have the nicest grandpa. One day Dad Petersen and I were sitting in the living room. I asked him, "Dad, how did you ever produce a wonderful daughter like Martha?" He smiled and said, "Charlie, you can do almost anything with a child if you love him enough." He was so right. Security and stability come most to those people who have been most loved in their homes.

Of course, there will be some punishment. But what is punishment? It can be either for correction or revenge. I believe it is the nature of God—both here and hereafter—to punish only for making better. I promise you that before I punish you, I will ask myself this question: "Am I punishing him for him—or am I punishing him for me?"

The Chinese have a proverb which says, "He who strikes the first blow has run out of ideas." I feel like that, Peter. For me, physical punishment is an admission of failure. It shows I haven't thought hard enough for better ideas. I don't mean that you will be over-indulged. It will be hard to draw the line, but whenever I don't know, I hope I will always err on the side of love.

Next, I promise you that I will never say "No" if I can possibly say "Yes."

We see it often. Babies raised in a positive atmosphere develop much better personalities than those who constantly hear the words "No," "Stop," "Don't."

Let me show you what I mean. This has to do with a dirty old bale of binder twine. When we moved from Nebraska to Oklahoma, we brought it along. I had used it there to tie sacks of feed and miscellaneous items. It cost something like $1.15. So I said, "Now, Philip, you see this binder twine? I want you to leave it alone." But it held a strange fascination for him and he began to use it any time he wanted. I would say, "Don't," "No," and "You can't!" But all to no avail.

That went on for six or eight months. Then one day I came home tired. There was the garage, looking like a no-man's land with binder twine across, back and forth, up and down. I had to cut my way through to get the car in. And was I provoked! I ground my teeth as I slashed at that binder twine. Suddenly, when I was halfway through the maze, a light dawned. I asked myself, "Why do you want this binder twine? What if Philip does use it?"

So when I went in to supper that night, Philip was there and I began, "Say, about that binder twine!" He hung his head and mumbled, "Yes, Daddy." Then I said, "Philip, I've changed my mind. You can use that old binder twine any time you want. What's more, all those tools out in the garage I've labelled 'No'—you go ahead and use them. I can buy new tools, but I can't buy new boys." There never was a sunrise like that smile. "Thanks, Daddy," he beamed. And guess what, Peter. He hasn't touched that binder twine since!

So there it is. I will say "Yes" every time I can. A positive background for a little boy—I hope I can give you that.

Here is my third promise: I pledge that I will really be with you when I am with you.

That may sound odd, but a little black-eyed lady in our church taught me a lesson. I was sympathizing with her one night because her husband was gone often. I said, "It must be hard to have him away from home." She smiled as she answered, "Some men don't have to be home much. What I mean is, when Ray is home, he's home!"

I sat with a young doctor recently. We were talking about this, and we decided that with people on schedules like ours, it's important to be present when we are present. For instance, a little boy said to me not long ago, "One thing I don't like at our house is the newspaper." As we discussed it, I understood. Every night his daddy comes home, props the newspaper in front of him, and says, "Now you go away till I finish the news." Peter, there never has been anything in the news; there never will be anything in the news; but that you are more important than the news.

Time is a problem with me, but you will be glad to know that we have one night a week at our house, called "Family Night." To people who call from distant places with, "Won't you give a speech at our banquet?" we say, "This is our night to lie on the floor and romp, to pop popcorn and play games." We also say it to our church committees. You know, Peter, I have never had anyone argue. They seem to understand.

Sometimes when I take trips you will go with me. We will stop at dime stores and buy balloons. And we will eat hamburgers. We will talk about things you want to talk about like, "Why isn't a cow green when it eats so much grass?" Or "What's inside a nail?" Or, "Is there really a man on the moon?" And sometimes if I come home and I'm tired (too bad we leave our worst behavior for those we love the most), I hope you will remind me that I promised—one Sunday before you were twelve hours old—I promised you, when I am home, I will *really* be home.

I pledge you also that I will try to see things from a child's point of view.

I learned something the other day, Peter. I was fixing the highchair for you. I was down on the floor, and supper was on the table. You know something? The mashed potatoes on Paul Jim's plate looked like a whole mountain of snow. Mother seemed to be a huge giant sitting there and Karen was certainly large for seven years. For just a moment I caught a glimpse of how things look to little eyes.

So when you come in shouting. "There's a cowboy pistol down at Danner's that makes smoke and I've got to have it right now," I promise you this. I will try to see things from your angle and arrive at a sensible answer.

One day I was in a restaurant and a little girl said, "Mommy, can I have another helping?" Her mother said, "No." Then the little girl asked, "Why not, Mommy?" And her mother answered, "Because I said so." Well now, I hope we will be able to talk and find some reasonable answers. So, I will try to see your point of view and not make the mistake of expecting you to be an adult too quickly. And, just as important, I hope I will not try to keep you a baby when you want to be an adult.

Comes now a small item, but very hard sometimes. I promise to be a good waiter.

We had a wonderful lady who took care of Philip, Karen, and Paul until she moved away. When she left, it was like a familiar tree going down outside the window. It left a hole in our landscape. Sometimes when we would scold your brothers or sister, she would say, "Ah, he's only little. Just let him grow. All he needs is a great big dose of waitin' on the Lord."

When your Cub Scout den mother calls and says that Peter has been naughty the last two meetings; when your teacher informs us that Peter is having trouble with his arithmetic; I hope I will be able to produce "a great big dose of waitin' on the Lord." So many things work out in time.

And here is the top promise. I will do everything I can to put your hand in the hand of your Heavenly Father.

I see many people with troubles—and numberless folks lost

in the high weeds. Yet I have never seen one of them but that their problem centers in this: They have lost their hold on the hand of God.

You see, Peter, you don't really belong to me. God put you here. What is a baby? Science says a baby is fourteen percent coal tar, nineteen percent calcium, eight percent phosphorus, eleven percent magnesium, and things like that. This is a baby. But some day you will be married and have a baby of your own. And when the woman you love holds that baby in her arms, you will know that anything as wonderful as a baby had to come from God.

I hope that I will be able to make religion natural to you. It is natural. In fact, I think this relationship with God is the only thing that *is* one hundred percent natural. We will pray together until it is easy for you to put your arms on the window sill of heaven and look into the face of God.

Before I put you back in your crib, I want to tell you something Philip said.

We had been out in the country for a ride. It was evening and we ran out of gas. We were walking along after we had been to the farm house, and I was carrying a can of gas. Philip was only four. He was playing along, throwing rocks at the telephone poles, picking flowers, and then, all of a sudden it got dark. Sometimes night comes all at once in the country. Philip came over, put his little hand in mine and said, "Take my hand, Daddy. I might get lost."

Peter, there is a hand reaching to you from the heart of the universe. If you will lay your hand in the hand of God and walk with Him, you will never ever get lost.

A Growing Self-Government

The more I encourage
my child to think for himself
the more he will care what I think!

One

"I've Got to Be Me!"

Question: What are parents for?

Answer: Parents are for helping sons and daughters achieve their God-given best.

If this is true, then one of my first jobs as a parent comes clear. I must say and mean it:

> Listen my children! Your first loyalty is not to me. You came by me, but you are not from me. In you there is a native self. The secret is to discover who God wants you to be and be true to that. This moment I set you free to say, "Get off my back. I've got to be me!"

"Self-actualization" is the rallying theme for a coming new breed of psychologists. Every man, they say, has an intrinsic nature which needs realization. The healthiest persons, according to them, are those who feel free to become themselves. Disease, ill-temper, tragedy, result from thwarting this innate being. (They don't discuss origin. They simply say it's there.)

By the very nature of our position as parents, we are inclined to over-push. We pour our little ones into molds of our making. We jam them with what we want them to become. We drive. We coerce. We bribe. We threaten. We live our broken dreams again as we hurry them toward the future.

We compare our product with neighbors, classmates, brothers, sisters, cousins, the boss's child. We measure by "What will people think?"

Over our shoulder, so many watchers watching.

Grandparents! They watch, adoring!

Aunt Doris. Like a hawk she watches. Her family already raised; each one so well married; such beautiful parents bringing up all those lovely children.

Those boring eggheads down the block. They are watching too. Their boring little eggheads bring home straight "A's."

From everywhere, there are eyes on us. The whole world seems to be focusing right here. And before we know it, we have forgotten who we are. Who we are, first, is human aids to some divine business. Our number one responsibility is not to shape this child. It is, more accurately, to preside over his shaping of himself.

> Blessed is the family where children are allowed to
> become what they can as fast as they can. Blessed also are
> the parents who, as fast as they can, will get out of
> the way!

Two

Three Goals to Self-Government

In our family we have a Credo for parent-child relationships. It is set on this principle which we believe to be basic:

> The more sensible self-government we allow at the right time, the better things will be all the time—better for the children—better for us—better for their future—better for ours!

Because we believe this, we have established some specific goals. We spell them out and lay them on the line for the whole family. There is no signing and sealing, but the agreement is clearly understood. These things are a definite part of our growing together. They are for real.

CREDO

> If we do our part to make you independent;
> if you respond with a growing maturity;
> if we together can pace these developments right;
> here are three specific aims of our family
> for your self-government.

Goal One

BY YOUR SENIOR YEAR IN HIGH SCHOOL YOU WILL BE MAKING ALL YOUR OWN RULES.

You will set your curfew

We will ask you to tell us what it is. We will expect you to use the phone when you will be late. Also when you stay overnight with someone, you will call. This will accommodate our sleep. It will make life less worrisome for both of us. But the time is yours to decide and we will respect your judgment.

You will go where you want to go

The only places off-limits are those you decide are off-limits. You will attend whatever parties you choose to attend. Because we like you, we will expect you at family events, unless we hear otherwise. You know that worshiping together is big with us. But this year church attendance, too, is optional for you.

You will choose your own friends without comment from us

Color of skin, length of hair, cleanliness of person, behavior habits—you decide who you date, who you're seen with, what kind of people you like. From all races and classes and sizes and shapes you will select your own friends.

You will be your own censor

Movies and pictures, magazines and books . . . you decide. Together, we have learned to evaluate the phoney and the real. Now you're on your own. We'll still be around, but that's not forever. The time has arrived for you to take over. They are your eyes. It's your head. What you take in is your responsibility.

You will set your own standards; make all decisions about your own behavior; shape your own character.

Smoking, drinking, sex, drugs—from here out what you do with these is up to you.

We have every confidence that you will handle yourself right. But if you should make some mistakes, remember this: we will not condemn or deride you. We will never point our finger or judge. Our attitude toward you will always be love with no reservations. You know we'll be in the wings. We will advise with you when you ask for our advice.

You will understand that parental habits of seventeen years die hard. We may slip. But you are free to turn us off any way you want. This includes your right to say, "Button your lip!" Of course, being mature, you will use mature terminology like: "Thank you for your advice. But I am now a senior. Remember?"

This is some kind of high goal. But we will do our best to get you ready for it if you do yours.

For sixteen years we will have been in a parent-child relationship. Now for twelve months we will enjoy you as an adult. This is what we've been aiming for—your launching into complete self-government.

Goal Two

BY YOUR JUNIOR YEAR IN HIGH SCHOOL WE WANT YOU TO TOTALLY MANAGE YOURSELF FINANCIALLY

As he comes out of junior high, the child moves toward a frustrating position financially. For years, he has been battered by advertising pitched directly to his age group. Every adjective from a boy's vocabulary has been harnessed to take him for a ride. Girls too!

Now our sons and daughters are sensing something new. Things they had accepted with little thought begin to register. There are down payments, monthly payments; big deals, bad deals, budgets, bills; interest, salaries, taxes, rent. These and dozens of other words with dollar signs come on strong. In any home they make up a large part of the family conversation.

The gang at our house tells us this can be almost too much. They appreciate some help here in understanding what it's about. All this mysterious talk needs bringing out of the abstract into the practical.

A few sessions on the family budget—intake—outgo—and "here's where you fit in" may be just the thing. It might even do more than show the child *his* place. One of our tribe, after such a pow-wow, came up with a classic. Obviously, he had seen more than his own position. What he said was, "Gee, Dad! Take care of yourself!"

Yet, because this is new, he does some tall wondering. He goes from these sessions to ask himself important questions: "Exactly how do I match my wants with the needs of everyone else around here? How much should I hope for, ask for, push for?"

There is one sure way to bring much of this mystery into focus. It is to move certain items in the budget and buying to the child's own management. By the ninth grade he has spent hours learning addition, subtraction, multiplication, division. Now, if we let him assume more of his own expenditures, an exciting thing happens. All that effort shapes up to a great new theme—"Arithmetic and *me!*"

At this point we hold some serious discussions on goal two of our Credo. We have been talking about it for a long time in general terms. Now the excitement begins to move closer. Loud and clear, we zero in on the year of the big takeover.

The agreement pointing toward this event says: "When you are sixteen we will turn over your own money management to you. Your allowance now will cover everything but your food and housing. As you approach your junior year, we will ask you to prepare a budget. It should cover your total needs. Clothes, cokes, haircuts; telephone, toiletries, dates; school expenditures, shows, recreation; gasoline, gifts, your personal needs. The works!

"You know our family motto: *Give ten percent. Save ten percent. Spend the rest with thanksgiving and praise.*

"We'll expect you to include your tithes, and save some money. After you have made your own estimates, we'll work it over together. We'll even add some for emergencies and miscellaneous. Practicing at home these two years you will become an expert in handling money.

"The word for that will be 'Congratulations to you!' One more indication that you have earned your parents' respect. We will be proud of you and your good judgment. Not everyone reaches such a high level of maturity by this age."

Credo-Goal Three is sweet music to teen ears! It sounds like wheels. Beautiful wheels!

Goal Three

BY DRIVER'S LICENSE AGE WE WANT YOU IN YOUR OWN CAR

"If you have proven yourself responsible, we make this compact with you: When you have completed driver's education, we'll start shopping. This will be one of our fifty-fifties. You pay half. We pay half. You decide when to start saving your money. Obviously, we're not thinking about an MG or a Stingray. Chances are you can't afford the latest model. But we'll scout for a used winner and match you dollar for dollar.

"Then there is an added item which sounds like economic bad news. It is. Your insurance may cost you as much as the car. We'll share that too, because it won't be much fun. But that's the way it is. Things nice to have around usually cost something extra to keep them around. Yet it will be worth it. The first big purchase is one of the great ones. And it's yours, because you have proven yourself ready!"

There are a couple of car happenings in our experience which may be worth reporting.

Many girls lack the motor-yen which is standard in young males. But some daughters do care, and ours did. For thirty days!

What actually took place is some kind of funny as we look back. Like her older brother she knew this was part of our self-government deal. So, when her turn came, she got her car. She baby-sat; giftwrapped at a jewelry store; did all kinds of odd jobs; and squirreled away for wheels.

It was a neat little coupe of considerable vintage. Excellent condition. (Amazing how many secondhand cars have been driven only by little old ladies to church on Sunday. That's what the salesmen said and we *were* lucky. Except for one. That little old lady must have driven only to the drag races on Sunday!)

But Karen's was a honey and she loved it. Madly she loved it for thirty days as a teenage daughter can love madly for thirty days. Then, almost to the hour, she announced, "Daddy, I have decided something. It is not necessary for me to have a car. I don't need a car. I don't want a car. I want you to sell my car!"

There were two reasons for this one hundred and eighty degree turnaround. First, and most important: "The boys don't ask me to ride with them anymore." Second: "———

asked me to drive her across town to see this cool guy and I measured—it was forty-eight miles altogether. Do you know what she gave me? One measly little quarter. How much did you say it costs to drive a car? Well, whatever it is, I'm sure it's more than a half-cent per mile! Right there I decided I'm being silly." Like she said, she really was being silly. *But she's the one who said it!*

So we sold her car.

The other item which probably should be mentioned concerns one of our boys. At driver's license age he decided he didn't want a car yet. He had saved his money too. Worked in a grocery store. Helped a painter. Set up banquet rooms in a big hotel. Scraped dishes in a restaurant. Mowed lawns. Plus other things. But when the time came he nixed the whole deal. Of course, we asked him why. To which, like many other things at this age, there was no clear answer. The nearest he could come was, "I just don't feel like I'm ready!" But there it is again—*he said it!*

Then twelve months after he got his driver's license we bought his car. Old, but oh boy, what a creampuff. This one *was* owned by a little old lady.

Peter is our most recent addition to the ranks of car owners. Thinking a teenager's thoughts might be helpful, I asked him some questions. (This was at breakfast, on purpose. At our house drawing anyone into conversation at this hour is something else. Usually we don't try. But when you want to know what really matters, this is the place. You mess around with various subjects. If you find somebody's hot button this early, you know it's a big deal.)

My question was, "Pete, why do you think a car by the Junior year is a good goal? Lots of parents would like it straight from a teen-ager. What does it do for you? Is there anything bad about it?"

Here are his answers translated into after-breakfast language for adults (no order intended):

> You don't have to bug your parents about going somewhere, like taking you to town to buy a notebook.
> It's nice to be able to do things for your mom, like going to the grocery, hauling your little brother and that. It saves her time and that's nice.
> You have to learn to save money for gas. What I mean is it fits in with giving the kid a chance to manage his own money.
> I like to take my friends places. This makes me feel good and it's nice for them.
> It makes it so I don't have to be afraid all the time of what my folks are thinking. I know they trust me and I don't worry if they are going to jump me about something.
> I think it's a natural part of self-government.

He never even mentioned what's bad about it, so I didn't push. Knowing him, I'm sure the only thing bad he could think would go like this, "It's bad that more kids don't have their own car at sixteen!"

Which just may be the truth. No one in his right mind would give tools for destruction to a juvenile. But what if we had the tools for making greater people and weren't using them? Perhaps some day a wiser generation of parents will know. Children have a tremendous capacity for growing up. Wise parents do everything wise to promote self-reliance!

Self-government in any of its forms needs some getting ready. This can start in infancy. At our house, one of its earliest applications comes with toilet training. We don't like messy children. Who does? But what if we win this battle and lose the war?

One mother we know boasted, "My Sybil is only eleven months old, and she's one hundred percent toilet trained." To which I can think of no better reply than Grandma Smithers, "Mine would of been too if I'd of kept 'em on the potty twenty-four hours a day."

Nobody knows for sure how this affects a child's future. Even the psychiatrists with their "anal" theories don't have all these answers. But we've seen enough to convince us. Over-pushiness, starting at the bathroom, is strictly no good. They do have to learn some time, that's for sure. But this is one world record we better forget. Beginning right here, the lean ought to be toward self-government.

Many of the same things can be said for eating. With us this has been a favorite theme. The biggest reason is our tendency to overweight, beginning with me.

My children used to say, "If we didn't have daddy, we'd have to keep a pig." To be sure (well almost sure) they said it with affection. But the message came through. I was a compulsive cleaner-upper. I licked my own plate clean. Then I roamed all over the table grazing on everyone else's left-overs.

It took some time to catch the culprit. What I was doing really, was repeating my childhood training. "Clean your plate" . . . "Every last bite" . . . "Eat up now!"

Some place down the line I had transferred that admonition to, "Clean the table of *everybody's* last bite." All of which is simply to note a tricky fact. We can get right confused, plus heavy, when we overdo at somebody else's food.

It was our family doctor who started us thinking about this. One night at a church dinner he gave it to us straight. We had been badgering our firstborn to lick his platter clean. The good doctor stood it as long as he could. Then, in a voice pitched with pathos for Phil, he said:

> Let me tell you something about the Lord and boys. What you don't know is, they're put together so they can get the message before we can. And if you don't understand me, what I mean is, he's being smart and you're not.

There's that self-government thing again. Of course, we should be sure they eat wholesome foods. There ought to be some regulations about sweets. Seven cookies before dinner could be a bit much. The same for little green apples and cokes unlimited.

So how can we be sure? The answer is that we can't. Like the Good Book puts it when it talks of love, "We know in part." But when we went to the mirror with the doctor's words, we saw it. We had been concentrating too much on what kind of parents we were. What we needed was a larger focus on who we were parents to.

Any family interested in self-government will be led to growing places of its own. Opportunities to apply these principles will present themselves all over the place.

Television: Can you depend on a twelve-year-old to regulate himself if you say, "Choose your own programs this year?"

Sleep: When do you finally tell them, "We're going to bed. You turn in when you think you should?"

Homework: Do you ever get to the place where you can trust the young mind this much? "About your schoolwork. We're through bugging you. If you pass, that's nice. If you make the honor roll, good show. If you fail, we'll love you. The time has come for you to do your own thing."

I'm not arguing for total permissiveness. But the more we studied the doctor's words the more they made sense. So we tried them on for size. Toilet, mealtime, everywhere we tested them thoroughly.

Amazing discovery! To our children's joy and our own, we decided he spoke the truth clearly: "THEY'RE PUT TOGETHER SO THEY CAN GET THE MESSAGE BEFORE WE CAN."

Three

Questions! Questions!

Query one: *Doesn't all this allowance by his Junior year make a child lazy?*

Answer: You may be in for a happy surprise!

The Lord put His sons and daughters together this way—the more they are allowed to manage their own money the more ambitious they become! In the handling of their funds, they discover new thrills. Earning, planning, spending; almost always these things stimulate more incentive.

Point worth a father's remembering: To tell my child how hard I labor is to beat the air. He never discovers the value of the earned dollar from my talking about mine. Only *his* earned dollar delivers the message. He learns about hard cash from working hard.

Query two: *My child is such a spendthrift. What if he blew it all at once? How could he ever control himself?*

The answer here will vary from another surprise to exactly what this parent is thinking. One daughter, like her folks feared, gathered all her friends at the malt shop. With one grand flourish, she blew her wad pronto.

Or it might even go in the opposite direction. Another child, because he had not been well prepared, did the reverse. He promptly froze all his assets and refused to spend anything.

All of which means that the average child needs help at the outset. Closer surveillance at first may save him embarrassment and launch the program more effectively. But from numerous tries seen in consultation, I'll bet on the average youngster to come through. Given half a chance, plus a bit of early help, he'll adjust.

He'll also be a happier child, which makes him nicer to live with. That, in turn, has another effect. His parents aren't quite so impossible to him. Maybe these characters can be lived with!

Query three: *What if we can't afford it?*

In certain situations, this is sure to be true. In which case some halfway program may be possible. Most children can sense it when their parents are having a rough time. But, however difficult the total picture, this is a fact—the solid high schooler will appreciate every bit of independence he is given. In most cases he will also rise to meet the challenges put to him. And if there isn't enough money, he'll understand it better from a position of trust.

In many cases parents come on another fact. They are already spending more on their children than they thought. Actually, the child spending on his own may save the family money.

Query four: *Would we dare begin now? How can I be sure we're ready for something like this? Can such a program be implemented at a late date?*

Answer: Lean to a "Yes."

The average Junior and Senior is too hemmed in during his final years at home. If he has a normal behavior record; if he has not been given to the bizarre; if he is at least in the middle group scholastically; he probably would respond well to a trial run at self-government.

Naturally, in homes not accustomed to it, planning is important. It will take considerable discussion and wise timing. Nobody's program can be applied without adaptation. Anything this different must be tailored to fit. But where parent and child came to it honestly trying, there have been some amazing results. Even adopted as a hurry-up corrective, it has often been the saving difference.

We've seen enough to stand on this statement: Introduced to new liberties, it's a good bet the teenager will suddenly blossom. And sometimes the most beautiful amazement comes in the hearts of his parents.

One mother tells it well. They had agreed to a trial run. In her own words she describes what happened:

> When we decided to let her live her way, we met a wonderful new person coming toward us. Do you know what we decided? All that buried goodness had to come from somewhere. Maybe we weren't such failures after all. We actually liked each other. Believe me, it was the most thrilling experience of our lives.

Four

Panic from Too Much Freedom

From readers of *The Stork is Dead* comes an avalanche of teen letters. They are spilling their inside trauma about sex and how to handle it. In an effort to keep some kind of order I file them by subject. One envelope is marked, "Panic Letters From Too Much Freedom."

Here is a typical plaint of a fourteen-year-old. Her agony, would you believe, is an overdose of self-government.

> My problem is one you probably don't hear much. My daddy is a doctor and he is so busy. My mother is a champion golfer and she is at the club every afternoon when I come home from school. On weekends they party and sometimes I worry about it that they drink so much, especially lately. But what really bothers me is how they let me do almost anything I want to. They never tell me when to come in and I can go anywhere. You might think how lucky she is. But I tell you that is not how I feel about it. What bothers me is I wonder if I am all that ready to decide everything by myself.

Too many restrictions are not good. Over-regulation leads to rebellion. But too few may be equally bad. Under-regulation produces a kind of low grade inner alarm.

We have concluded at our house that children want only so much self-government. They secretly hope we will not give them more than they can handle. At any given age they do better if they are sure of this—those parental reins are held in firm hands!

In a recent family conference on the theme, Peter made an interesting observation. "Dad," he said, "sometimes it makes me feel good when you get tough and say, 'Your options have now expired! The answer is No'!"

So we moved from that to, "When does he want us to say this?" Two big places came through:

When we think he is about to hurt himself.

He wants firm parental control then. Can he be sure we will safeguard his present and his future? At some ages he is a threat to himself and he knows it. His security at these times comes from an inner certainty that we know it too.

When we think he is about to hurt others.

He wants us to move in then. At certain stages he could care less about the rest of the world. Yet, secretly, he hopes we will protect him from damaging others. Brothers, sisters, parents, friends could get hurt. He doesn't want that. On occasion everyone of us goes fifty-one percent "mad" at the world. It helps to know in our heat that someone loves us this much: they will apply their cool to our raging. Every child I have known intimately appreciates that from his home. I even like it as an adult.

That is a beautiful phrase from the Twenty-third Psalm, "Thy rod and thy staff, they comfort me." These were hard things. They were not paper-mache. Tools of protection must be made of solid stuff. Sometimes they hurt. But, like the Psalmist says, they comfort too.

As Peter's father, I have a special place in the family's firmness. I can be strong and still be gentle. In *Letters to Philip* * the opening chapter is built on the motto: "Wherever dad sits is the head of the table!"

I get some interesting mail about that. There are many these days who hold that everything in the home should be fifty-fifty. I don't buy it. That man who handles his paternal authority deftly will be loved for it. His woman will appreciate him more.

So will his children.

* Charlie W. Shedd, *Letters to Philip* (New York: Doubleday and Company, Inc., 1968).

Five

Principles of Discipline

Like the maid said, "You don't get nothin' for nothin' but nothin'."

At its best, discipline is preparation for life at its best. Whether it is diver diving, dancer dancing, singer singing; that's how it is. Same for the painter painting, and the kicker of field goals. Flyer of space ships; doctor operating; conductor conducting; "hot lips" at his trumpet; pole vaulter flowing over the bar—attached to all things done well, there is a high price tag. But even this can be confusing. How much pressure is just enough? How much is too much?

We have found that our family does better with some specified guidelines on discipline and punishment. These have been a good thing for us:

Whenever we discipline our children it should be for them and not for us.

These words from the original "Promises to Peter" still hold: "I believe it is the nature of God—both here and hereafter—to punish only to make better."

And I need to be careful who I am trying to better. I could be overconcerned to succeed through my offspring. Unless I guard it, I may be projecting my broken dreams into my child's performance. Am I trying to create a showpiece to compensate for my own frustrations? Do I care too much what others think of my product?

I should also set up special guards when I am emotionally exhausted. If I am angry at anyone, I may take it out here. This is particularly true if someone with authority over me has been wearing me thin.

Too tired, too busy, too hurried; at times like these I can make serious mistakes. It takes some kind of special dedication to ask (with hand raised to strike), "Is this for my child or for me?"

All discipline and punishment should be to help my child be his best. It should never come out of the second-rate me.

That child will most respect his parents' authority whose parents have treated him with respect.

"I demand respect!"

So, what else is news?

The news is that respect is not to be had on demand.

Lofty goal: I want my child to respect me because he has decided I am respectable!

When his behavior is bad, I must downgrade the action rather than him. "Don't be a fool!" is not as effective as, "What you are about to do looks foolish to me!" There is a big difference between "I think you're stupid!" and "I think what you did is stupid!" One attacks the person. The other preserves the person's dignity.

Always, he will respect me more if I treat him with respect.

We will value the person above the thing.

My favorite memory of my father calls up the importance of this. We were driving in Des Moines, Iowa. It was before the day of Driver Education and he was teaching me.

My first lessons were in the country. But this was something different. Cars buzzing; swervers in and out; big trucks behind and before; busses turning into our lane of traffic; all very grim to a small-town novice!

At the crest of my panic, I looked over and saw my dad grinning.

"Don't worry, son," he said. "If they take our fenders, we'll get some more!"

I didn't fully appreciate it then. But I have many times since. I knew my dad was a nut about his car. But there was one thing more important. My feelings mattered more than the fenders!

Whether it is a "totalled" late model automobile, a chipped eighteenth century heirloom, or the broken mirror—I must never put material things ahead of my child.

Sure we should have some limits. If he wants to burn down the school or punch out his sister's eyes; if he is kicking the cat or twisting the dog's ears to make him yelp; I better step in. There are places where he must be taught respect for things and people. But, whether it is binder twine or tools in the rain, the same thing applies. Nothing puts a child down quite like being devalued to a thing!

Whatever the punishment, get it over fast. Then forget it.

Cutting allowances for six weeks is too long. Grounding for thirty days . . . same thing. All dragging reminders are ineffective. They create slow burn. Slow burn creates resentment.

Thirty days for a boy is like forever. One week without phone privileges for a girl feels like, "I'm in for life." He is a "now" guy. She is all "today." These are the years of low visibility. Their wants are immediate. They are not equipped to understand that "this too shall pass."

When the seething lingers, they may push it down inside to

forget it. But does it forget them? One day it might return, and what have we gained if our punishment backfires? If the final outcome is more grievous than the original misdemeanor, who wins?

But timing is not all. Having served his sentence, there is another thing our child wants to know. Will we put the memory where it belongs? Are we willing to seal our lips now and turn to the future?

We should have an understanding about discussions outside our home. Any humiliating recall, coming back from outside the family is double deadly. We are not likely to be soon forgiven if we slip here. Dredging up past mistakes for review is bad business. Anytime, anywhere, this is no good.

So, whatever the punishment; no matter the discipline; when the wrong has been laid to rest and the mourning subsides, this is the epitaph and it is beautiful, "FORGET IT."

The best kind of discipline is that in which the child has a voice.

We may get good behavior faster if we operate from a position of unquestionable authority. But it won't be as healthy nor as lasting!

We may also get rapid results by threat. But this, too, is likely to be temporary. (If we do threaten, we better be prepared to carry it out. We lose something if we don't.)

We find it often works to let the child assist in the rule making. Giving him a voice goes especially well when parents cannot agree. Why not take it up in family session? "This time we admit we're puzzled. Let's work it out together." Naturally this shouldn't be overdone. It could be too heavy as a regular thing. But regulated, it offers a nice variety, plus a happy surprise. And one surprise is that the child usually leans toward more discipline rather than less. There's that question again: Does he sense how much correction he needs? Yet there is never any question about this—in our family we always come out of these sessions with a new sense of togetherness.

Flash! If my children are as smart as I like to think, it stands to reason—their brains added to mine should be better than mine alone!

Six

"If I Hit You, Run!"

"He who strikes the first blow has run out of ideas." This Chinese proverb from the original "Promises to Peter" has served us well for sixteen years.

Early in our parenthood we took the pledge—*no spankings!* And to be sure we wouldn't turn back, we said to our small fry: "Now hear this! We are through forever with swatting and switching and all general clobbering. There has to be some better way than bare hand on bare derriere. We don't know for sure what, but we'll work out something together. And whatever it is, it won't be physical. So, we kid you not. If ever we start to hit, you run like crazy. We've gone temporarily out of our minds."

To which from the general public comes a chorus of "What do you mean 'temporarily'? What are you, some kind of subversive or something?"

Whenever we talk on parenthood, here's where the egg hits the fan. Spanking is one of those borderline holies. "You must be putting us on! Are you questioning the ancient rite of the laying on of hands (or articles too numerous to mention)?

This is like voting on things you don't vote on. Everybody in favor of God, say 'I'."

We know it's a fact. The decision never to strike may come from some neurotic trend in our backgrounds. He who has been whipped knows the trauma it can produce. And he also knows another thing. He sometimes was punished all out of proportion to his misdemeanor.

This is one of the reasons why we think there must be a better way: *Physical punishment lends itself too easily to the venting of adult frustrations.*

People who lost their tempers, or the ones who made us lose ours; the idiot who swerved in ahead of us in the traffic line; the vice-president with his foot in our face; that bitchy neighbor whose specialty is making mountains out of molehills; dozens of others from today and hundreds from our ancient history; what do they have to do with it? Maybe plenty.

And even if we could bar our door to this ugly array, that isn't all.

There is also the steady emotional drag of family life itself. Nervous tension, disappointment, money worries, illness—these sap our energy. Yesterday someone in the family said something which hurt. Today someone didn't say something and that hurt even more. Phones ringing, parents shouting, Susie pouting, company coming, bills arriving, Johnny griping, "Where did you leave my socks?" Dad yelling "for heaven's sake turn it down". . . . etcetera, etcetera, etcetera *ad-infinitum,* ad-a-bunch!

These and a thousand other things can drive us straight up our mortgaged walls.

Certain strong and steady souls may take this all in stride. Then there are others of us who find it almost too much some days. Inside us lurks this temptation to what the psychologists call "transference." Which, being interpreted could mean, "Look out, Junior. Run!"

There is a second reason why we don't like physical punishment: *it too often leads to confusion*. In us, in the child, and all over the place—confusion.

Everyone knows the old saw, "This hurts me more than it hurts you." But, strange switch here, that is exactly what happened at our house. Before we swore off, it too often came out this way—we felt awful and the kids felt fine, thank you!

Which, say the child guidance experts, may be exactly what's wrong. Spanking and switching and belting around makes it too easy.

Most parents hope to produce a healthy conscience in their children. And that takes time. Not only time over a period of years but time right now in thinking things through. Suppose the child begins to count on the harsher forms to "make things right again." Could we be depriving him of an all-important growing place?

Meanwhile, back on the adult front, the weak get weaker. Did we do right? Were we too harsh? Did he deserve that much? Are we sure we were punishing him for him? So, being uncertain, we are tempted now. Should we pour on the love to close this chasm? How much? When? In what way?

To which questions come the same monotonous answer: Nobody knows. And when nobody knows, the result is more confusion. Confusion here. Confusion there. Everywhere confusion.

There is one good thing to be said for physical punishment: It's speedier. Which in itself may look like something it isn't. Most parents learn the hard way. These smart youngsters of ours, have some uncanny methods of putting it to us. They send forth their dove. They hold out the white flag. And we, being so anxious for peace, welcome their signals like crazy. Then one day we discover to our chagrin that we have been taken again. There is a kind of peace here all right. But it's a perimeter peace. Down where the action is, the war is still on. What we won was only an outer precinct.

All of which leaves us looking straight into the searching eyes of an inescapable conclusion—the crucial test of whatever method we use is not external. "Honest to goodness" goodness is an inside job.

Question: Is what we are doing together making him want to be good, really good, at the core?

Seven

"So, What Can We Do?"

If only we had some kind of parental computer. Feed your problem in right here, punch the button, presto! See the happy, foolproof answers. Color them beautiful.

Or maybe a pill for control of the bad things. One for the big problems. Two for the little things—like adolescence, menopause, and daddy just got fired. Three now and then for kicks. They're good for what ails you, and if nothing ails you, they're good for that too.

But since there is no computer, no pill, no easy way, what can we do?

The best swing and swat substitute we know is what our family calls "Plus Marks." It is the foundation of several things. What it covers is each child's share of the family income plus these other matters—work and discipline and punishment.

We planned it with our first two children. They loved it and so did we. We still do. So do they. Likewise the three who came later. And we all agree this was great for us.

(Which may be worth a side comment. Our children usually like best what they had a part in. Even the ones who missed the launching go for it more if they know this: they may not have been there in the beginning, but they were represented.)

"Plus Marks" features a big blackboard in the kitchen. On it, written large, is the name of each child. And opposite each name is a certain number of plus marks, each worth five cents. The minimum number is five and we begin at age three, four, or kindergarten. Some say this is much too young. Can a child get with it if he doesn't understand mathematics? We don't know. But we know each of our gang says some of his earliest impressions focus here. When does a child store up happy memories for later recall? When does he sense his rights and obligations? That we can't tell either. But we began early and we think it's a good time for beginning.

Like I was saying, "Plus Marks" covers our work program. We'll take a close look at that in another chapter. Here, let's limit our treatment to how it applies for the hard things.

The way this works is that each individual receives a graduated number of plus marks. Suppose now your child is eight and he gets ten plus marks. Payment is made on Saturday. Fifty cents, plus whatever else he's earned extra. (More on this in the Work section.) That's his allowance for the week.

Now here comes the hooker. Up there on the big board opposite his name there may be some minus marks. And each minus mark subtracts one nickel.

By now you get the swing of it. Extra plus marks are awarded for extra work. Minus marks go on the board for misbehavior.

Who decides how many for what? Usually mom or dad, but sometimes the family votes if there is a disagreement. If you got a bad deal and want to risk appeal, go ahead. You might win. But if other members of the family think you got off too lightly, watch out. They might hang it on you.

This always has one walloping good effect. Nobody needs to

sit still for punishment if he feels he was treated unfairly. He can bring it before the jury, argue his case, and take his chances. Which more often than not is worth his trouble. If nothing else, he's had a chance to say his say.

Question: If you believe in majority rule, couldn't this be dangerous? When there are more than two children, isn't it possible for them to overthrow parents?

Answer: Yes, under this system it could happen.

But here is an interesting memory. In twenty-plus years, there were very few reversals. And of the few we remember clearly, we recall another thing—the young voters were right and we were wrong!

So there are some risks. But we'll take our chances because for our clan there also are some beautiful things here . . . "Elasticity" . . . "Democracy" . . . "Excitement" . . . "Justice" . . . "Fun" . . . "Togetherness."

Another item or two might be worth a think on punishment and plus marks.

1. That board up there for everyone's view seems to say so many things. One is, "Payday *does* come!" But if you've messed yourself up with minuses, God is good. Come Saturday we start over. Love those new beginnings!

2. Perhaps the most potent punch of our plus marks is how it works in public. Most families these days mingle. Group events, dinner engagements, affairs too numerous to mention, they are all a part of our package. Which for us as parents is always a special challenge. Sometimes our children behave away, and act up only at home. But sometimes, pray for us, they reverse the procedure. And when this does happen, we find our system some kind of extra effective.

Suppose this is such a day. One of our very normal offspring is doing his Caesar routine. This is the one where he starts out impossible and gradually gets worse. When everyone, including us, can stand him no more, we have this whammy. Here we call him aside. Now we say with quiet ardor, "My dear whoozit! You either knock it off this very minute or else. And the else is five big minus marks."

"Blackmail! Plain blackmail!" Which, if that's what it is for you, then you would never use it. But if you're not yet quite that holy; if you like to settle things fast sometimes so nobody knows what happened; if you're a dynamite guy at heart, but you just can't stand the explosion; then you simply must try plus marks. For which, if your bunch is like ours, they will thank you now and forever.

Here are some quotes direct from those who have been through it:

> I have one friend whose parents keep changing their minds. They promise and then they forget or they say he misunderstood. With plus marks there can't be any argument. You know for sure. . . . What you mean is it's so neat and clean. It's definite!

> It does away with jealousy. When somebody is getting more than you are, it's because he's older and you'll get that much when you're his age. So you don't resent it. . . . That's right, and I think this is one thing that stops a lot of fighting. It's fair and you know everybody is getting a square deal.

> I feel like it taught me to think before I did something. . . . Yeah man! You got nobody but yourself to blame!

> At some of my friends' houses they yell at each other all the time. This way you don't have to. . . . It seems as if you can understand each other better. You can see what kind of a week everybody is having and this gives you more sympathy.

> You know what I like best? It makes sort of a fun thing out of work and chores and other things you don't like. . . . Well, I never thought of it as fun, but it sure keeps things interesting.

Here is another method of discipline we like: *"I'LL GIVE YOU TEN"*

This one goes on like a hammerlock.

Usually the strong-armer is dad, but not always. Even a one hundred pound woman can make it work if she handles it right. Meaning, at the right time, in the right place, and not too often.

Whichever parent is the doer, entry is by ultimatum: "I'll give you ten to . . . pick up those toys . . . quit teasing your sister . . . return the books to the bookcase . . . give the ball back," or anything fitting the category, "You better stop," "You better start," "You better not," "You better . . ." Then comes the "one! two! three!" delivered in solemn tone at sober pace.

Question: What happens if child does not straighten up by ten?

Answer: Occasionally, over the years, we've met other parents who said, "Oh, we do that too!" (A couple of top sergeant types said they count to three—good idea for little ones—the joint might be a shambles by ten. Then there was one parent who said he used the age of the child involved. "I'll give you till eleven!" does seem to add a bit, doesn't it? Or it might if we were eleven.)

Now comes the amazing thing. Whenever we met these fellow-paralyzers, we would ask, "What do you do if you get no response?" Would you believe? Everyone of them has said the same thing, "We don't know! It's *always* worked!"

Same here. In twenty years not one of ours ever challenged the system. And if you knew a couple of these characters, you'd know it's a winner.

So we don't know what we'd do, because we've never had to do it. But you can bet we'd do something. What? The only answer we know is this lovely bit of King James: "It would be given unto us in that hour!"

"But ours are two and three! All this self-government talk sounds great. I can hardly wait. But with little ones, what can we do?"

Good question. When ours were two and three, I could hardly wait either. In our family, this has to be the most awful age of man. Girls too! Every morning at this stage, I thanked God I was the father. And I hesitate to say it, but maybe I should. There were days when I hoped the office load would keep me late. Like till after their bedtime!

The reason why I almost held back is this bit of discouraging news—with our self-government philosophy these years right here are sometimes ghastly. In fact that is so true we came to a cruel and brilliant deduction: The best solution is to bury them at two and dig them up when they're five.

We are not a permissive family, as I hope you've sensed. We do not believe in, "Let us deal lightly with Junior lest we warp his little personality." What we do believe in is self-management, self-control, self-discipline, self-government. And we believe in that amount which any child can handle at any given age.

But at two and three this is an unknown factor. We are not trained child psychologists educated at the best schools. We do not know all that is going on inside these midget monsters. (Nor, I confess, have we read anyone else who knows for gilt-edge-guaranteed-certain.) So this is a guessing game partly. How much is too much? How much is not enough? How much is just right?

We don't know that either. But we did agree to some guidance principles which we clung to. (And "clung" is the right word. This is where our "no physical punishment" really got tested.)

These guidelines were rather like mountains we could look up to now and then. It gave us strength to know that something was still standing.

We even cut our ideas down to four words for ready reference: "Prevention," "Ventilation," "Isolation," "Re-attachment."

Prevention takes time. Unfortunately, it often takes that time when time is at a premium. "Company coming!" has a way of tightening everyone. Plus everything, including the schedule. But wise planning may allow for a few moments of reading, playing, walking, talking. Even the littlest person responds well to a bit of this: "There are other people in our lives but this very minute you are most important." Which may be all the seeding some hurricanes need to scatter their would-be damage.

Whenever they're upset by other people around; when they're tired from things which make small bodies tired; when they want to dally and poke and we're steaming ahead; it takes some kind of bigness to see things through their eyes. But learning to do it might prevent agony later.

Two "sayings" have blessed us as we struggled with this discipline. The first is a line from one of my own books: "On numerous occasions the interrupter is more important than the interrupted." * Number two is from The Book: "Provoke not thy children to wrath."

Ventilation in our vocabulary of discipline means, "Don't cut him off too soon. He may need blowing more than correcting." A lot of things are better off "Out" than "In." So if there's no one around, we tend in this direction: "Open up all the pipes, kid! Scream on. Let go!"

But if it's all too much, the locale is *Isolation*. Too much is (a) when he's better off alone and we're better off without him; (b) when it could be dangerous to the furnishings and stuff, including people; (c) when we can't think of anything else.

And how this goes might be in any one of four directions. Philip was no sooner in his cell than he began having a ball. Fun things. Singing, reading, drawing, playing, listening to records. Whatever it took to convince him that life could be beautiful again, that's what he did.

Karen threw everything in sight. And I do mean everything. If it wasn't nailed down, glued down, fastened down, look out. We finally settled on a bathroom; moved everything throwable; then prayed the plumbing would outlast her. Which it did.

Paul refused to stay put. Fortunately, at that time we had a narrow hall so escape was not easy. But we usually had to

---

* Charlie W. Shedd *Time for All Things,* Ten Affirmations on the Christian Use of Time (Nashville: Abingdon Press, 1962), p. 68.

stand at the door until his storms abated. Thank heaven, with him it didn't last long. But standing there hanging on to the doorknob, we would ask, *"Who's* being punished?" Knowing him in all his present brilliance, we can't help wondering—was he thinking what we were thinking and with great glee?

The last two took it normally. (Guess we're getting somewhere.) They simply sobbed it through and came out when it was over.

Which is the moment for that all-important *Reattachment.* What this consists of is whatever it takes to say, "I love you! I love you! I love you!" Usually this means holding, patting, stroking; any such gesture to cover his ebbing agony. But however it's done, it's basic. This is one of the pillars of a child's security. He knows he isn't always loveable. But is he always loved?

We must get it across—"You can never do anything so dreadful; say anything so terrible; be anything so awful, but that we still love you!"

Before we wind this down on methods, there is one thing more you might like. I almost decided not to tell you, because it does sound strange. Yet since we all need whatever help we can get, this is the story.

I know a mother who, when her children are impossible, disappears. She's not gone long. Usually, it's a few seconds, two or three minutes. At first her husband thought it was some kind of special weakness. There are those who simply can't take fighting and bickering and general combat.

Of course, he became concerned. Who wants to be left on the battlefield? One alone against the hosts of evil is no fun. So he decided he'd investigate. And when he put a tracer on her, this is what he found. At the pitch of conflict she would go to their bedroom; shut the door; stay there briefly; and then return to take up the fray again.

Only now he observed a strange thing. Often when she got back, there wasn't any fray. It was as if she had gone somewhere to call long distance. Had she been in touch with Someone who had some pull somehow? Whatever she did, the man knew this for sure; it was worth doing.

Then one day he asked her secret. So help me, here's what the lady said: "What I do is quiet myself and talk to the Lord a little. I tell Him whatever I think He should know. Then I ask Him if I must discipline, to help me do it right. Over the long run, I find this works better. It's safer than moving right in on my own and I like what happens all around."

So do I.

As methods go, I just had to say—in one husband's opinion, this is the ultimate in beautiful!

Eight

"Is He Positive or Negative?"

"Sometimes I'm good.
Sometimes I'm bad.
Oh yes, Lord."

There is a school of thought which says that man is neither positive nor negative. Rather he is born with tendencies either way.

Then there are the heavies who say it isn't so. Man is innately sinful. "Original Sin" is the church's label for this condition. Into which morass I do not intend to lead you. Except to say that nobody I've heard, read, or met knows exactly what all it means.

John Calvin gave it a good try. At least he said he understood what he meant. The way he pinned it on the wall left little doubt. He called it "total depravity." But his biographers tell us Calvin had kidney stones. The which, if you've had one, should be explanation enough for his intensity. Nobody with kidney stones regularly could be optimistic about anything.

There is also a simpering kind of sweetness and light philosophy. Everything is just dandy, thank you! Man is all good. Woman too. Whatever we call bad is but a figment of our imagination, or something. If you smashed your index finger in the car door this morning, beam on! Think of the nine good ones.

Sometimes it seems to us the smart thing is to quit trying to be so smart. What we concluded was that old Omar said a real thing, "Myself when young did eagerly frequent Doctor and Saint, and heard great argument: but evermore came out by the same door wherein I went."

So one day we decided for ourselves. Let the preachers of doom say on. Let the sin experts glower. We would settle this thing for ourselves.

Questions for Charlie and Martha as parents:

> Is our first responsibility to keep the badness from getting out of hand?
>
> Is our number one job to free the innate fineness already there?

We asked ourselves these things and prayed and waited. Then it came through loud and clear. These particular children of ours *were* something special. We could *feel* it. This positive data came from Headquarters. At least it was Headquarters for us, and where else should young parents begin?

Then we got another message. These children came to us with some inborn capacities. Things like knowing their own needs sometimes before anyone, including us. We must also teach them to depend on their inner timetable, very accurate.

This will be surprising news to the average child, but it is good news. Somehow, by our words and our dealing we need to declare it: "You are wonderfully put together. God made you. He knows what He wants from you. If you will learn to listen, He will guide you. We want you to understand this: It is more important that you do what He wants than what we want. Our aim is to clear the lines for your communication first with Him."

Then when we got this message through and really meant it, we discovered something else. The Lord also made children like this: They care more what their parents think, the more their parents let them think for themselves.

Certainly there should be suggestions and a helping hand. There must also be some "You better not's" and "You betters." "I wouldn't," "You shouldn't," "Don't," "No," "Never": there must be some of these. So, too, the Ten Commandments and some special ones of our own.

But the more we get it turned in this direction, the more another commandment comes through. This one is for us and it isn't easy.

Commandment:

THOU SHALT NOT FRUSTRATE THE HOLY IN THY CHILD!

I shall not fling
My strong, my deadly noose of years
About the neck of youth,
Nor with my flagging life and graying hairs
Tether him from his choice.
But, smiling, I shall free him,
Remembering anew
The swift, keen whir of hope,
The tensing muscle, the ecstatic breath
With which, long, long ago
I leapt into the race.
And though he run an alien course
I shall not call him back—I shall rejoice.

Author unknown

Lessons in How to Love

From somewhere, if we are to survive, we must produce a people who know how to love.

One

Father-Mother Love

Essay from an eleven-year-old boy:

> My mother keeps a cookie jar in the kitchen and we can help ourselves except we can't if it is too close to meal time. Only my dad can any time. When he comes home from the office, he helps himself no matter if it is just before we eat. He always slaps my mother on the behind and brags about how great she is and how good she can cook. Then she turns around and they hug. The way they do it you would think they just got married or something. It makes me feel good. This is what I like best about my home.

Suppose we could give one gift to every child in the world. What should it be? Education? Enough to eat? Freedom from fear? Money? Fun? A career with that all-important sense of worth?

Good as these are there is one thing better. According to those who know, this is a fact: the most favored children in the world are the ones whose parents love each other!

In the original *Promises to Peter* my first pledge was, "I will remember always that it takes a lot of love to make good children." What I had in mind then was love between father and son. But in the years which followed, my horizons grew.

It was a doctor who first lifted my sights. I had been elected to the board of a fine psychiatric hospital. Here I became acquainted with brilliant men. They knew amazing things about the human mind. So I listened. Then one day in a symposium on child development I heard a new thing. The lecturer was a famous pre-adolescent psychiatrist. His typically over-worded subject was: "Importance of Parental Harmony as the Primary Source of Emotional Stability in the Growing Child."

Of course, I applied what was said to Peter. And this is how it came through: *the greatest thing I could do for my boy was to love his mother well!*

That wouldn't be news for some people. But I regret to report that up until then I had never given it a thought. And when I began to ponder this insight, I discovered an awful truth —Peter's dad was a lousy lover!

It wasn't that I didn't love his mother. It was simply that I had let that fact be crowded out by other facts. There really were dozens of calls on my time . . . pastor of a large church . . . administrative matters stacked high . . . speaking engagements . . . counselling, counselling . . . committees, committees, ad nauseam.

That's how it was. Here the man sat with some promises to his new-born. And the one thing he needed most wasn't there.

When there is only one thing to do, that is the thing to do. It wasn't easy but it was essential. So I delivered the message and the message was:

> Martha, you are the most! You are the greatest
> happening of my life. But I doubt if you really know it.

> My performance diminishes my words. I've been going like mad and I've been rationalizing, but now I see. You would rather I do things *with* you than *for* you. So, from now on, you're number one. We must take time for each other, *first!*

We worked out a simple two-point program and dedicated ourselves to its accomplishment. I can tell you it was the wisest thing I ever did. She says it's big with her too.

How it goes is like this:

Once a week out together for dinner alone!

No guests. No entertaining. This is our dinner date for each other only. Sometimes it's lunch. But wherever and whenever, we put our elbows on the table for a deep look. Far down into each other's souls we look.

This date is a sacred trust. Fifty-two times a year. No exceptions. Our children know it and they love it. Come Saturday if we haven't had our date, they remind us. So we leave them to their hamburgers and we take off together for "our" time.

"But how can we do this during the early years when our income barely stretches?" The only answer we know is to make it a top item on the budget. Some things never get done unless they are placed high on the agenda and kept there.

There may be those who say, "But should you schedule your love? Aren't these things you would do naturally?" Maybe they are, and if that's how you are, great. But here are two people who know from experience, it takes time to love right! And in today's fast world any safeguard to that end is worth what it takes.

Fifteen minutes a day visiting in depth.

Most couples would assume they communicate that much. Do they? In depth? We're not talking here about the bills, the children's problems, or planning the weekend picnic. The subject now is, "What's going on inside Martha and Charlie."

Much of our praying is done in these moments. Here we separate the real from fantasy; test things we've been reading; discuss our growing worries; share our mutual hopes; surface our hostilities. Usually, of course, the fifteen minutes carries over; sometimes way over.

Such communication requires careful development through the years. The moral courage to be fully honest does not come quickly. Neither is it easy. But it does make for inner quiet.

We usually do this on our love seat. Nice—a rocking two-place divan without which it wouldn't be home. When the children see us together here, they get the message.

"Let us go softly. These two are attending a delicate business."

The child whose father and mother love each other is not preoccupied with worry. Life is good. The past has been good. The future will be good. He lives with greater expectancy.

That preadolescent psychiatrist in his paper said some other things. One was that the child of quarreling parents is almost sure to feel guilty. Because the human mind is what it is, he turns their trauma in on himself. . . . "Am I the cause of their conflict". . . . "Did I do something wrong?". . . . "Would they have been better off without me?" But this kind of false guilt can only be destructive. It is strictly no good.

Sexually also, the child of parents in love has a better chance. At a certain stage, a strange thing happens. The child hopes, plans, plots for exclusive rights to the opposite parent. Why? Just because that's how God made them. The little girl wants her father to herself. The boy sees his dad as a rival for his mother's love. When does this happen? How long does it last? There are almost as many answers as there are children. But when they finally realize this wall is impregnable, they accept it. Now they move back onto the road of their natural development. And unless this happens, the confusion could be disastrous. Homosexuality, lesbianism, and other twisted ideas may originate here.

Nobody knows for sure all that goes on in the close-in emotional interchange at home. But we do know this. Hostility between two people spills over into the lives of those around them. Bitterness cannot be contained by the bitter. Always this ugly seepage is an inevitable part of hatred.

We hear it often in the consultation room: "We're staying together just for the children!" But children won't be fooled. No matter how hard we try to disguise, they get the true message. Parents smart enough to camouflage should be smart enough to grasp this fact: Children from *unresolved* parental conflict are invariably damaged.

So, said the wise man, it's a fortunate child whose parents love with a healthy love. Guess he's right. One of our sons puts it in his own words:

> When I was younger, I didn't realize why your taking Mom out to eat alone made me feel so good. But it was like one of the many reassuring signs of the love between you. I can remember the jolt I felt the first time I heard you say that you loved each other *more* than any of us kids. I can also remember thinking that out and realizing how fortunate it is. After all, we are products of that love. So seeing it expressed was bound to make us all the more secure.*

---

* We remember also that first time we discussed this grim subject. It was at "interesting things" in our dinner devotions. "Who do you love most? Us, or each other?" That is one delicate question for family discussion, isn't it? But our policy has always been, "Anyone can bring up anything." So they asked and wouldn't give up. "But our love for each other is a different kind of love than our love for you" wouldn't do. They kept pushing, driving for a decision. If you could sit in on one of these

events, you'd know it's a fact. Arguing one theme to a frazzle is no unusual thing here. They finally got around to the "situational" thing. "If you had to choose between, etc!" That's when we levelled with them. "Yes, the love of parent for child *is* different. But if you've got to have a decision, there is no stronger love than ours for each other." That, I remember is how we put it. Which kind of family soirée I have never discussed with my psychiatrist friends. They might not like it. As a matter of fact, we weren't even sure we liked it. But every one of our children did. No exception. As another one said, "At first it seemed like my world was coming apart when I heard you say that. But after I thought it over, I felt like everything fit together again good."

Two

A Positive Idea of God

Does Peter believe in God?

Crucial matter.

But even more important is another question: *"What kind of God does Peter believe in?"*

My son will not walk hand-in-hand with God, because I say he should. He may fake it for a time, because he knows the folks expect this. But whether it's genuine and how long it lasts is not my decision. That's his.

And what determines whether this is for real?

Comes now a truth which is almost too much!

Psychologists say that what Peter thinks of his Heavenly Father will largely be determined by what he thinks of me!

From his mother, my son learns about people. From her, consciously and unconsciously, his mind is at work shaping its attitudes toward others . . . bad/good . . . kind/cruel . . . strong/weak . . . Constantly he watches. He evaluates these mother-reactions. He applies them to the people in his own life. Naturally he takes some people-feelings from his dad. Yet under normal circumstance this is minimized by mother-proximity.

But, say the experts, in a religiously-oriented family something else is taking place. From his father-feelings the child is shaping his concept of God.

It can hardly be otherwise. Very young, he learns to repeat the familiar prayer, "Our Father who art in heaven." Then if he goes to church, he will be hearing both wise and foolish things on "Your loving heavenly Father." Down the road he will be taught some hard-to-understand doctrines about "Father, Son, and Holy Spirit."

Being a smart youngster he ponders this, studies, contemplates. . . . "My father is unkind. . . . my father is too busy. . . . my father is not dependable. . . . my father is stern." If his father-thoughts must be that negative, this could be devastating.

Religiously speaking, many people do not like God. They cannot feel good about Him. They don't know why. Could the reason be traced to this failure? No one has taught them the all-important mental process of CONTRAST!

So one day when the time is right I must say to my son:

> God is your Heavenly Father and you can be glad that's true. I am your earthly father. But there is a big difference. Your Heavenly Father is like a perfect Father. But since I am not, you must learn to contrast. Whenever I am the right kind of father, that's how God is. But whenever I am not, God is the opposite. Unless you remember this, you might not like God."

(Warning—the more "pious" the father, the more church-centered, Bible-carrying, moralistic, the more this must be made clear.)

I have known people who said they were atheists. Yet as they discussed their negative concepts, an interesting fact came clear. It wasn't their minds which turned them off. It was what they had been through. Some hurt in their heart had moved them away from God. They were emotional atheists. Whatever happened had left them with an inadequate deity. As I got to know them, I understood. If I had to believe like they believed, I wouldn't believe either. Better not to believe in God than to count on a God like theirs. And it is amazing how often these people surface negative father relationships!

Uncanny fact: In discussing these poor father-memories, almost always their descriptions clustered around such terms as STERN! SEVERE! DEMANDING! DISTANT! CRUEL! BUSY! BUSY! BUSY!

Which leads me to think I better be about the business of knowing the God of love.

How else can I keep my pledge from the original "Promises to Peter"? . . . "I will do everything I can to put your hand in the hand of God."

Three

Calamities Are Fifty-Fifty

Among our most meaningful family practices is what we call 50–50 on calamities. How this goes is that dad pays half the cost for a childhood mistake.

What does this mean?

Timothy borrows neighbor girl's new skates. With a front drive like ours a bit of pre-dinner skating is very inviting. That is, if you don't leave the skates where the new pup gets to them. Beautiful red straps. Irresistible to a dog. But what good are skates without straps? If only new straps would make them the same again. But they won't. These are the built-in kind. Sure we could get them patched back together. But this wouldn't be fair to Nancy Lee. There is no other way. New skates, $4.08. . . . Timothy, $2.04; Dad, $2.04.

Peter is waiting on Ken to pick him up for their tennis date. A few practice balls batted against the house might sharpen that backhand. Unless, of course, one ball sails through front window. Cost: $8.36. (Fortunately it's a small one.) Dad's half: $4.18.

Karen mistakenly parks her car in tow-away zone at Houston City Library. Cost: $30.00. Dad pays $15.00.

Paul knocks his baseball through Manfield's bedroom window. Cost of new window: $18.10. Cost to dad: $9.05.

Philip gets speeding ticket. Fine: $26.80. Dad's share: $13.40.

The reasoning behind this procedure:

You are my child. I am responsible for what you do. Whenever you lay an egg, it could be partially my fault. I've tried to teach you to think. It is inevitable that in part you gather your action data from me.

You made a mistake. It is only fair that I help you discharge the obligation of your error. Besides, with us what happens to one, happens to all. Families are for sharing each other's burdens. "Love rejoices not at wrong but rejoices in the right." So we must make things right together.

But just one minute here! Couldn't a parent taking on half these costs make his child careless? As a matter of fact, the exact opposite happens. Or at least it has with us.

The reason? Maybe it's because God put us together this way. When we have experienced His mercy personally, we love Him that much more.

There is little else to say. The one-ness which comes from this kind of sharing cannot be described. It can only be felt.

So, this is one of my greatest challenges as a dad: That my child may learn what his Heavenly Father is like from me!

Four

The Fun Family Devotions

There are two attitudes toward any religion. One is "the-duty-of" performance. The other is "the-joy-of" doing. At our house exuberance is all important in family worship. Without this, the whole thing becomes a drag.

For us the fun of it is tied up in what we call "interesting things." By vote of the family each member reserves time immediately following evening dinner. But the worship begins as the meal starts.

The first person (designated by dad) reports on his most interesting experience during the last twenty-four hours. This may include something unusual which happened to him or his friends . . . a surprisingly good grade . . . the home-run that won the ball game . . . a compliment . . . the unexpected letter . . . some wonder of nature . . . the place where he felt God closest . . . big breaks . . . bad breaks . . . little breaks in the routine . . . somebody's trauma . . . an aching heart . . . something read . . . what a friend said—humorous, sad, sharp . . . maybe a complaint . . . or a deal for the family's voting . . . the good, the bad, the ugly; any of these will do.

Each person takes his turn around the table. Although no one is permitted to repeat what has been said before, new slants and different versions are acceptable. When each has had his turn, seconds and thirds are admissible. All this leads to many questions, plus considerable traffic in ideas.

Several good things come from this practice.

Each person opens up his soul a bit for all to see what's going on inside. During the "cave" years this is particularly important. (In the early teens our children seemed to withdraw for a time. We call these the "cave" years.) Since there is a twenty-five cent fine for the nonparticipant, everyone makes a noble effort. Those who wonder where the fine money goes, will be interested in this: it has been so long since anyone had to pay, no one can remember. Families who feel a dearth of intercommunication will find "interesting things" a powerful stimulant.

Serendipity is another plus for this method. The Persian tale has it that those Princes of Serendip were forever reading life for surprises. The practice of "interesting things" in our devotional base has affected us like that. We live with expectancy. Life's goodness is likely to leap at us from any person or behind any thing. Each day is vibrant with meaning. The goodness of God is never far away.

"Interesting things" also keeps the family conversation where it should be—positive. Stewed teacher, fried neighbors, roast relatives are not the healthiest fare. Criticism, judging, gossip—maybe these are no threat in other homes. But they are with us.

It is not that we don't face facts. We are not out to create a bunch of simpering Pollyanna's. Still, we want our gang to know the good as well as the bad. And that seems to take some doing. We have never gotten so holy but that evil seems always at hand.

Family worship closes with readings from a selected devotional. Material chosen may vary from the Bible (children's versions preferred) to almost anything. Perhaps it is the devotional guide of some denomination. Maybe it's a piece chosen from the leader's other reading. It might be a book of meditations. Turns are taken in order by members of the family. Then we hold hands as the leader says the closing prayer. Sometimes he requests a period of silence, sentence prayers, the Lord's prayer.

We also hold hands during the blessing which is said whenever someone thinks of it. "Saying grace" is a must for some people at the outset. It seems more authentic at our table if there is something in the inner man. We like it better that way and we think the Lord does too.

Our devotional policy is "hang loose." Since duty is often a spoiler, we do better with plenty of leeway. Karen's important date; Phil's ham radio meeting; that horn honking for Paul; Peter's ball game; Timmy's drum lesson; these have a way of closing in fast on the schedule. This is particularly true if interesting things have led to a lengthy discussion. So at times like this, we may say a quick prayer and let that do it. We have even been known to close on this note, "The Lord knows we're busy tonight. Pray on the way."

It should be explained that a fun devotions is only one of four goals for our family at prayer. Others are: A daily quiet time for each member; father and mother in a duet of prayer before God; a covenant wherein each member of the family agrees to pray daily for every other member.

As usual in this tribe, the key word with all these things is stretch. When? By what manner? How long? These are optional. There is no checking, no prying, no examination. Each person is on his own to do it his way.

We did agree at the outset to observe family worship fifty-one percent of the time. At first this required special effort from all of us. Today, as we move closer to daily, there is no question in anyone's mind about this—whatever the method, by any procedure, the more we pray, the better it goes.

Five

Lessons in Democracy

"Mr. Chairman, I make a motion" . . . "I second it" . . . "The floor is now open for discussion" . . . "It seems to me" . . . "But you said" . . . "That's not what I meant" . . . "I make a substitute motion" . . . "Point of order" . . . "But it says in Robert's Rules" . . . "Can I make a substitute to the substitute?" . . . "What you mean is an addenda to the addenda" . . . "Snow again, kid, I didn't get your drift" . . . "All right, I'm going to call the original motion" . . . "Whoa Billy! Exactly what are we voting on?" . . . "Question! Question!" . . . "All in favor say 'I' " . . . "Those opposed 'no' " . . . "The motion is carried!"

Sounds like fun? It is. But it's a whole lot more than that. This is one family doing an important thing together. What they are about is learning respect for a particular form of government. And there are some of us who think this is crucial business.

We have found that the more things we let our family vote on, the better. This is usually done at the evening meal in conjunction with "interesting things." And almost anything goes: What to name the new cat. . . . Which program will we see on T.V.? . . . . Can we watch during the meal tonight? . . . . Where shall we spend vacation? . . . . Shall we run from the hurricane or stay? . . . . Shall we take Karen's friend with us to the rodeo or go alone? . . . . We think the whole family should settle our difference of opinion. Whose turn is it to mow the lawn? . . . . We have $10.00 extra in our tithe. Where shall we give it? . . . . Are mom and dad right on grounding for the weekend? . . . . Shall we raise the allowances all around this year? . . . . How about taking in a movie, or shall we go swimming? . . . . What to name the other new cat.

One thing going here is the child learning his place in relation to everyone else. As parents, one of our chief responsibilities is to create a healthy "otherness" in our children. Is anything on the national scene more important than this?

From all over the place come the cries of the young rebels—"I want my freedom." The raucous noise from some of them means, "I want mine. To hell with yours!"

Some of the young could care less about democracy, because nobody has shown them its value. Somebody failed to drive the point home. Always our freedom has obligations to the freedom of others. Our kind of freedom is not freedom *from.* It is freedom *for.*

There is little hope for the future unless someone gets the message through—how to blend with the whole; how to give in to the law when that is best for all concerned; how to control one's anger when the vote goes the other way; how to change the law by due process.

Question: Whose job is it to do this training?
Answer: Parents.

Basically this will either get done in the home or it won't get done. And great civilizations have collapsed when one generation forgot to teach another what made the system strong.

Will our nation survive? And if she doesn't, could it be because too many parents neglected this—to teach their children some valuable lessons in democracy at home?

Six

People Are to Love!

Word from Timothy, twelve!

"Do you remember Franklin? The thing I couldn't stand about him was how he only pretended to like me so he could use my toys. I don't think you should do that.

"And another thing I think you ought to know about is the way kids feel when their parents ask them to run errands all the time. Sometimes they like to do it, but sometimes they have other things to do or they don't feel like it. If you would tell him why you want him to do it, it would be better. Like if you are too tired to go get the paper, why don't you tell him that's why? Maybe he is tired too. Or if he is busy watching something important on television, tell him he can go get it when the program is over.

"And if you can't wait that long, then you should tell him why you can't wait or go get it yourself. Sometimes I feel like saying what they do at Uncle Herly's house, 'Who was your servant before I came?' "

Hmmmm! Maybe I should reexamine one thing I have always taught my children.

"Remember gang," I say with great gusto, "THINGS ARE TO USE! PEOPLE ARE TO LOVE!"

Seven

Honesty

"There is a great big huge lion out in our yard."

That's what he said. Which might have been all right under ordinary circumstances. But this was the day of his mother's bridge club.

You know how that is. Sometimes with the public you can't let certain things pass. Particularly, if they deal with the family image, you can't.

So, glancing out the window, she saw the neighbor's yellow cat. Large cat all right, but no lion.

"Warren," she said, "You know we don't tell lies at our house."

Then with a bit of added flourish, she sent him to his room.

What else could you do with the bridge club watching? And even then, have we covered all the rules of good motherhood?

Ordinarily, when we are wondering what people will say, we say too much. This was one of those times.

For whatever reason she put on this extra touch: "Maybe it would be a good idea if you had a talk with the Lord about that!"

In less time than it takes to say, "Heavenly Father, Amen," Warren was back.

"Well," said one of the extroverts, "That was quick. What did God tell you?"

"Oh," answered the grinning youngster, "He said, 'Don't worry, Warren. When I first saw it, I thought it was a lion too.' "

Most of us would say she had it coming. Some things from the parents' side are better overlooked.

Fantasy may be one of these.

Every child needs some make-believe. It exercises his imagination. "Such stuff as dreams are made of" could become one of his strongest assets. Many good things were launched at the pad of somebody's fancy.

Pretend playmates can serve well. "Goalee Ga," "Moo Mee," "Barby-Shop-Twice-A-Month" make excellent company. These and a bunch of others came and went at our house. Each did his job (or was it "hers" or "its"?) for the right stretch of time. They filled the loneliness; entertained; educated our little ones in that all-important inner dialogue.

> So here is our deal, gang! Thoughts are the most interesting things coming and going around here. And some of the way-out ones are the most enjoyable. Let's have an understanding. We'll let you in on our fun things and you let us in on yours. The rule is: If you feel like sharing it, share it. We might even discover some good things together.

Under this compact we have two understandings; (a) we will not scorn (b) we will laugh *with* but never *at!*

"Interesting things" at our family table is often made more interesting by this agreement. Plus some fine things which were shaped by the family together out of somebody's day-dream.

The key words are, "*If* you feel like sharing it." This usually acts as the only necessary control. Sure, we have had some embarrassing moments, but few which couldn't be handled. This is our experience: Given a normal home and a normal child, the make-believe normally takes care of itself.

In addition we have learned that fantasy-sharing is one road to later honesty. Some of the communication gap between parent and youth may be closed before it happens. One way is to develop whatever techniques keep the roads open from infancy up.

Lying is something else. This bears closer scrutiny. But even here things may go better with some elasticity.

Most children will prevaricate a bit, if only for experiment. At first, and unless it develops into habit, the wise parent does not become hysterical. In the self-government home this type of dishonesty usually provides its own remedy.

Serious continuation bearing on life-style may need professional attention. But when the child realizes he is free to think *for* himself another thing happens. He begins to care more what he thinks *of* himself!

One aid to verbal honesty may be to level with the tribe about family skeletons. Wise parents tell children where the bodies are buried along the trail. This is particularly important with the "unmentionables." Premarriage pregnancies; Uncle Lester's prison term for embezzlement; why Aunt Grace hasn't spoken to Aunt Mabel in eleven years; generally, these and other items which could cause later concern should be handled calmly at home. At the proper time they can be put in the family talk stream as a natural part of living. Often it is the fuzzy unknowns which give us the fidgets.

Most children will be shaken enough without adding to their tremors. If an outsider tells them things they should have heard from us, they resent this. "Why didn't somebody clue me in? Can't I trust these people? What else is under the tombstones?"

This kind of anxiety is both destructive and unnecessary. It is also a deterrent to openess down the road.

The principle is: We will be as honest as we can with our children about everything! The more honest we are now the more honest they will be with us later.

Some kind of pre-think may also serve us well for *stealing*. Many parents come unglued when this happens. Yet here, too, the first times go better with the soft touch.

Unless there is some special aggravation, we can count on this rectifying itself. After we have given him an adequate allowance, we can trust the future. His growing self-respect from a growing self-government will do what needs doing. Always, anything we do in the home should be built on this premise—respectable performance from our children will come when our children can respect themselves.

But whatever shape the problems of dishonesty take, one thing needs doing. Somehow we must get the message through.

Love begins with self-love or it doesn't begin!

That's how we're made. Inner dishonesty fouls up our responses.

Which means that we must teach our children everything we can about self-analysis. At every age they must be shown that many things start at the mirror.

Some way I want my boy to get this. Self-honesty is the foundation for a solid tomorrow. This makes things right for us, for the groups we move in, for our one-to-one relationships. And it all begins with love for the self God meant us to be.

Which leads me to one real toughie. It is a hard fact I must face. *My children will probably be no more honest than I am.* Truth is one of those things where children learn more by osmosis than by words.

So what can I do? One difficult answer is to say and mean it—

> Peter, I need your help to help me be honest. In me there are things not to my liking. So, whenever you catch me lying or stealing or cutting some corners, I want you to lovingly stop me. Privately, never in public, you can help me. I will be forever grateful for everything you do to make your dad a better man. Thank you!

Bold step! Yes! But whenever a parent takes this step sincerely, another thing happens.

He is now in a position to talk.

He can talk about honesty and self-analysis and genuine love.

And his voice has the ring of truth and he will be heard!

Eight

"They Never Gave Us a Moment's Trouble"

Every now and then we hear some parent say, "She was the perfect child!" "He never gave us a moment's worry!" "Our children were always such a delight!"

Question: Are there really families like that?

Answer: Yes! But, unfortunately the "Yes" group includes: (a) well-regimented homes producing boxes of snakes to be dealt with later; (b) zombies who tread the dull road of compliance forever—and is there any sadder sight than a child whose emotions are distortions of his parent's problems in miniature?

At our house it is more likely to be ups and downs, ins and outs, "I love you" . . . "I hate you!" Yet the Lord is good in many ways. One of His ways is that He clouds unpleasant memories as He brings the nice things front and center.

Would you believe? Two of our children are married now, doing a job of living like we never did at their age. And for the life of us we can hardly remember anything bad.

"They were such a delight."

"Never gave us a moment's trouble!"

Nine

"Dear Charlie: I Hate You! Love, Martha"

It was a big surprise the day she left that note. It stopped me in my tracks. It shook me like nothing had till then.

But not any more. From that moment in our early marriage, we have learned this truth: Anger dredged up from down inside makes more room for genuine affection.

My child needs to know this too. There is sure to be some ambivalence in close relationships. Healthy parent-child feelings are not all sweetness and light.

One day, when he can comprehend it, I must say to Peter:

> You can't honestly like until you have honestly faced what you don't like. There will be times when you'll be angry at your mother and dad. There will also be flashes when we can hardly stand you. Don't panic. The key is not to avoid all negatives. It is to face them, receive them intelligently, and surface them respectably. If you keep your cool, this can make life interesting.

One of the finest examples I have seen of this happened recently in a pleasant suburban home. I was calling here because this family had attended our church. Father was there with the children. Mother had gone for what he called "her Saturday afternoon out." Right there I might have known these were some kind of unusual relationships.

As we sat visiting, I was in direct line with the picture window. Outside at the curb several scheming young things were plotting their pitch. The convertible trunk was heavy with surfboards.

Then a lovely Junior Higher came bounding in with her question. "Daddy, dear," she began. But noticing me, she hesitated. After proper introductions, she started again.

"Daddy," she said minus the lovey-dove, "The girls are going to Galveston surfing. Can I go? We'll have hamburgers on the beach and be back before ten." Etcetera . . . at great length . . . well oiled . . . thoroughly thought through from her side.

To which father replied, "I'm busy right now. We'll talk about it later."

(Which incidentally is murder for preachers. If you care about your child's religion, don't ever do that. With God all things are possible. But there is no reason to make it more difficult.)

Then having made with the usual "glad to meet you" fib, she took exit. Out front there was no small putting of heads together for the next effort. Whereupon she reappeared with fresh arguments well fortified. To which, same answer.

Cutting across three more single forays, let us now move to the double thrust. On this particular trip she brought an older friend. This one must have been barely driver's license age, especially attractive.

It will mean more here if you know another thing. Galveston and this nice house are some seventy miles apart. Excellent road. Freeway. Minimum speed, forty. Maximum, much more.

To say that our new adversary was a superb contender is

putting it mildly. If she wasn't on the debate team, she belonged there. Opening all the stops, she gave it her blonde, blue-eyed, swivel-hipped-best. This was the final pitch, designed for the closing.

Buddha sat unmoved. "I told you," said he (cool, like dry ice), "We will talk about it later."

Believe me, it was the final nail in my coffin. This time the looks were lethal, like "Drop Dead!"

Still she wasn't quite through. As she took her leave, our heroine turned. Peering from behind the safety of those big hallway pillars, she spat it out, "Daddy, sometimes I just hate you!"

Whereupon I thought I heard a new sound. It was like the brush of wings. The angels must have been bending low for his reply. And I tell you no lie. Twitching not, nor unfolding his arms, the "Chair" replied, "Darling, sometimes the feeling is one hundred percent mutual!"

For those who have never faced facts, this kind of thing comes as a shocker. But when we do a rerun, the word comes through like something else—truth! The mature family has learned to accept this. We won't love to the maximum one hundred percent of the time, nor do we need to.

Teaching a child to accept hostility is not all done by words. It might go better by demonstration. Particularly, lessons in how to love women need special attention. The father who cares can get this through as his sons study him with their mother. Then when they have seen the soft touch, he can say:

> Your mother is not perfect. She will make some mistakes and you may get caught in one of these. Now you can learn a good thing. You won't always agree with your woman. But you better know how to disagree with respect. The directions for here read, "Handle with care!"

As my sons well know, I am some kind of a nut at this point. Most boys would become better husbands with more specific education for it. I think the average man could love more thoroughly if he had been trained how to do it.

We also believe the family needs frequent discussion on the whole subject of relationships. It can be fun and it can be time well spent. For people close in; for those outside the home; for the ones we must deal with now and in the future; we have some special themes for some great discussions. One of these we call: "EIGHT THINGS TO REMEMBER IN MAD MOMENTS."

1. *Learn the signals;* yours and the other guy's. Maybe he's tired. Or hungry? Is she disappointed? Sick? You might avert real trouble by studying these things.

2. *Am I acting or reacting?* Am I losing my temper because he lost his? Psychologists call this "hooking my child." Good question: Will I go down to his level or bring him up to mine?

3. *Timing is all important.* Mature anger has a long fuse. Some things take care of themselves when we delay reaction. And what if they do get worse? A postponed response is usually better.

4. *If you can honestly agree somewhere, start there.* Look for glimmers of truth on his side. Make these your starting place. You'll more likely win your points if he knows you've seen his.

5. *Drop your voice.* Little secret for big help—in angry moments, lower your volume. A soft answer may disarm your antagonist. It takes him by surprise. This is something new. It can be good. Usually when any human being is angry, every fresh thought brings a blessing.

6. *Avoid ridicule, sarcasm, scorn, mimicry.* These never advance your cause. If you really want to settle the problem, you never do it by putting the other person down. (Once more to parents: "We gain nothing when we demean our children in their own eyes!")

7. *Develop some friends to serve as receivers.* Always, your anger is better out than in. Great relationships include the right to show the ugly self, too. This is our deal: "Home is the place for explosion. Because we love you, we will also love you in hostility. So, when you feel the need of it, splatter your 'mad' over the whole family."

Principle: When a child is angry, the broader the reaction screen, the better.

8. *Apology is for the great people.* The art of discharging our social obligations includes making amends. We do a fine thing for our children when we teach them: "You must learn to say, 'I'm sorry' with meaning. Hostility has not been fully handled until it has expressed regrets with sincerity."

This too is better caught than taught. It is usually one great day when a parent says, "I was wrong. I apologize!"

These "Eight Things to Remember for Mad Moments" have served us well. They have brought us to an important conclusion: One of the nicest things we can do is to let our loved ones be unlovely. And one of our jobs as parents is to train them how not to be nice, nicely!

Ten

Principles of Sex Education

Less than five percent of our nation's homes are doing an effective job in sex education.

Question: What is an effective job?

Answer: Whatever gives a child adequate information by the time he needs it.

Since publication of *The Stork is Dead,* I have talked *to* and *with* thousands of teenagers. Frequently, it is my practice to test groups where I am speaking. I ask them to close their eyes so no one is embarrassed by his answer. I explain that I am going to ask one question several different ways. Then I give them time to think, and ask for a show of hands. The questions are: Do you feel you got all you needed to know

Editor's Note: Dr. Shedd has purposely limited his discussion of sex in *You Can Be a Great Parent!* to avoid repetition from his earlier book *The Stork Is Dead.*

An immediate bestseller, *The Stork Is Dead,* grew out of a dialogue through correspondence with more than twenty thousand teenagers . . . readers of his columns in *Teen* magazine on sex and dating. This is the frankest book on sex yet, written for teenagers in a language they can understand and believe. But enthusiam for *The Stork Is Dead* has not been limited to teenagers—parents, medical doctors, educators, ministers, and psychologists have acclaimed it one of the most helpful and useful books on sex published to date. FWT about sex from your home? . . . . Do you think your mother and father did an adequate job of training you about sex? . . . . Could you go to your parents with any questions you'd like to ask on this subject?

"Please hold up your hand if you can answer yes to any of these." In ghetto and plush suburb; in small town and large cities; in fashionable private schools where students have everything money can buy; in orphan homes where they barely have what they need; in meetings of more than six thousand; with small groups; in all these settings, I've asked them. And in no case has the total number of raised hands been more than five percent!

To be specific the last three groups at different age levels were: One hundred and twenty-four Junior Highers in California, six affirmatives. Fifteen hundred High Schoolers in Texas, eighteen hands. Three hundred students at a Georgia College, eight.

These statistics were not selected to make a point. They are simply the last three. But there is little variance anywhere. *My conclusion is that our generation has miserably failed at sex education.* Which means that today's youth differ little here from those who have gone before. They join the long parade of ill-informed who were uninformed from the right sources.

Some day, will a wiser people do this job like it ought to be done—open and clean and early enough?

Which leads to the first of several principles of sex education in the home. Sources here are teenagers who got it straight and parents who gave it that way. From these, four basics:

1. *Sex education begins the day our child is born.* Nobody knows for sure how much a baby learns by feeling. Most authorities contend it is a great deal more than we suspect. But

whatever the early emotional pick-up, they all agree here—exhibit "A" of good relationships, mother and father, creates the finest emotional platform. As the little one matures, he senses a good thing going. He likes what he feels. This is solid and warm and mysterious. Nice!

2. *It is better to tell the child too much too soon than too little too late.* Parents often say, "But my child never asks questions." Neither do several million others. So wise parents don't wait. They stay alert. They move in at every opening. That pregnant mother down the block; the dog with her puppies; the cat and her kittens; colts; calves; rabbits; any other newborn thing may offer an opportunity. And if these never come, the opening should be made at the right time.

Those who wonder when that is, when to be specific, should know this—by eleven or twelve today (sometimes much earlier), sex talk is rushing in from every direction. Much of this is not good material. Some of it is very bad. This being true, the question better be faced: Do I want my child to get his sex training from others or from me?

Conclusion: That child is best prepared if he gets his sex education from mature sources who (a) do it lovingly, (b) do it soon enough, (c) do it thoroughly—meaning complete explanations of both good and bad.

If father isn't paralyzed by sex talk, he should take the lead. This goes for both boys and girls. Most men have the feeling that a daughter's sex education should be left entirely to her mother. That is not true. She also needs the male viewpoint. Those girls I know who seem most secure had some straight talk from dad. In an ideal situation the whole family discusses these things as a unit. This kind of togetherness, however, is very rare. And even then some person-to-person sessions go well.

Usually communication at its finest has a long history. I have already cited the importance of time alone with the child at an early age. Sex talk has a clearer ring against a background of much discussion about many things.

The parent who fears over-educating too early can put his worries aside. Children come ready equipped with an inside computer. It separates good from bad and stores for later use. But we make a serious mistake when we let someone outside the home start it going.

3. *Talk first about what's smart, not right and wrong.* "I don't care whether it's wrong. I want to know whether it's smart. Now don't give me your old religious pitch. Hell fire and sex has had it. I'm looking for some adult who will cool his moral fever long enough to tell me, 'What's smart for me.' "

These opening words from *The Stork is Dead* summarize the thinking of a whole generation. Most of today's gang has turned off "The Establishment." For them the God squad has had it!

Because this is true, we do well to stick to intelligence as our main beat. It isn't that we must never talk about morals. After we have their attention, we can bring them back to consider the basics. Having eliminated the pontificals, we can now say, " 'Smart' and 'Right' are put out by the same maker. What's 'wise' and what's 'good' go together forever. That's the way God did it. To which you and what you do are no exception!"

Provided we have earned the right to be heard, our children will listen. But we earn that right by time spent over a long period; by an example in love; and by beginning where they are.

4. They also listen to this: *"Great sex is not a happening. It's a creation. It is always smart to take a long look.* This is a do-it

yourself job. Twenty years from now your sex will be what you made it. Uninhibited love is great, but it isn't free. So keep your cool till the time is right. You will be glad you did."

Those who wonder if modern youth tunes in to these concepts, will appreciate this letter:

Dear Dr. Shedd:

This is the first time I ever wrote to someone like you but I felt like I had to tell you something. My parents gave me *The Stork is Dead* and I want you to know what it did for me.

My boy friend and I have gone together for two years. He is so great and I really do love him. We will probably get married some day but that is a long time yet. I am a senior in high school and he is a freshman at college studying to be a coach.

You know how it is when you love somebody so much. You keep getting closer and closer. So what happened is that I promised him I would go all the way when he comes home at the semester. That is when his birthday is.

But when I read your book, suddenly it came to me different. Now I realized how great sex can be if you wait and what you could do to yourself and lots of other people. So I wrote him and told him I was sorry but my promise was off.

Then do you know what happened? He wrote me back and said he was really glad I had decided that. What if I had gone ahead? I wonder what he would be thinking really and how would I feel?

That is what I wanted you to know and I just had to say thank you.

Love,

———

Eleven

Twenty Questions

Following publication of *Letters to Karen* and *Letters to Philip* I had this exciting invitation. *Teen* magazine asked me to write a column for them on "Sex and Dating." From this came the thousands of letters to which my editor refers.

In the months which followed I have been in constant communication with the youth world. I have spoken to seminars, camps, conferences, rallies, retreats, assemblies, bull sessions. I have talked with hundreds of teenagers by phone and face to face. And I can't think of any better way to describe my feeling than the words of Ezekiel: "I sat where they sat and remained there astonished among them." *

My publisher and I have worked out a format which we use in our presentations. It is designed to get the group doing its own thing as quickly as possible. Each person is given a blank card on which he is invited to write his question. These are anonymous. They are brought forward to a teen panel which groups them and selects the most representative.

From this background and my letters, here are the most asked questions in order of their frequency:

* Ezekiel 3:15, King James Version.

1. "Why shouldn't we go all the way?" . . . . "What's wrong with sex before marriage?" . . . . "If two people are sure they're in love, how could it be so bad like everyone says?"

2. "How far is still safe?" . . . . "What's the difference between necking and petting?" (The term "petting" to the teenager covers a wide range. Reference to "serious petting" often indicates mutual masturbation. This is much more common than most adults want to believe.)

3. "Is masturbation harmful?" . . . . "I heard this awful thing would happen if I keep doing it. Is that true?" (Scratch almost any teenager. Not far below the surface are some masturbation worries.)

4. "What kind of birth control do you recommend?" . . . . "Is the pill safe?" . . . . "How about the rhythm method?" . . . . "Is there any way to be absolutely sure?"

5. The pregnancy questions: "Do you think a couple should get married just because the girl is having a baby?" . . . . "I have this friend who is pregnant. What should I tell her?" (often meaning, "I am") . . . . "If I got this girl pregnant, what do you think I should do?" . . . . Then come the totally honest who always get me right here: "I'm pregnant. Please, help me."

6. "How can I say 'No' to this boy? I like him so much and he keeps begging me." . . . . "My boy friend says it isn't healthy to get so excited and not do it. Is that true?" . . . . "He says if I loved him I would let him". . . . . Other versions: "Everyone in our school does it". . . . . "How can I be popular unless I do?" . . . . (Those interested in discussing these

things thoroughly in the family circle are referred to: "Ways to Say 'No' " from *The Stork is Dead.*)

7. The Abortion questions: "Is abortion safe?" . . . . "Do you think they should legalize abortion?" . . . . "My girl friend says she is going to get an abortion. Where can I tell her to go?" (often meaning, "I got this girl pregnant and I'm in a jam.")

8. "What is married sex like?" . . . . "How often do they do it?" . . . . "Do they always do it the same way?"

9. "Do you think I will be forgiven for what I did?" . . . . "We didn't mean to. It just happened. We both feel terrible about it. How can we ever feel right again?" ("Forgiveness," "Mercy," "The Road Back"—to these themes there is no turning off the establishment. At this point the crowd listens 100% to 100% religion.)

10. "How can we stop?" . . . . "We've been doing it but we're trying to quit." . . . . "We can call it off for a little while and then it happens again." . . . . "Do you know any way for us not to do it again?"

(Note—out of the first ten questions, five come from the ones who are having intercourse!)

11. "How can I find out about sex?" . . . . "My folks never told me a thing. What should I do?" . . . . "Why do adults clam up whenever anyone mentions sex?" . . . . "I feel so stupid!" I think there are lots of things I don't know that I should."

12. The "It isn't fair" questions: "Do you think the double standard is right?" . . . . "My girl friend got pregnant and

now her boy friend has gone off and left her. I don't think that is very nice, do you?" . . . . "How can boys tell so much? He said it would be beautiful and he would always love me. So I let him and now he is bragging all over school. I am so embarrassed I could die. I don't see how boys can be like that."

The situations here come in endless variety. Which the wise parent will recognize as a prime opportunity for (a) impressing on boys their male responsibility (b) impressing on girls the truth that some sex facts are stacked against them. Adequate sex education for daughters will include plenty on the theme, "Wake up and smell the coffee, darling! You're never a little bit pregnant, and when you are, it's not him, but you!" This is tough talk. But if ever a generation of girls needed some of it, with love, this is it.

13. The "Going Steady" questions: "Why won't they let me go steady?" . . . . "My folks are so narrow minded. They accuse me of all kinds of things just because I never date anyone else but Johnny. What is the matter with them anyway?" . . . . "My dad said I can't date any boy twice in a row. Isn't that stupid?" . . . . "My parents make me double date all the time. I think that is so dumb. How can I get them to understand?"

14. The Marriage theme: "How can you tell if it's really love?" . . . . "When will I know whether this is the one for me?" . . . . "Do you ever know for sure, I mean that honest-to-goodness-no-wondering feeling?" . . . . "Can you help me decide about this girl I'm going with? There are some things I like very much about her. But sometimes I wonder about other things. If you could help me decide, it sure would help" . . . . "My boy friend says he knows for sure he is in love but I can't make up my mind. Can you tell me how to be certain?" (It is amazing how many homes include little or no

discussion on these things. Hours for planning the wedding. Plus hundreds of dollars. Zero for thoughts on marriage. Is this what the man meant—"Whom the gods would destroy they first make mad?" And is it this dearth of background which brings so many to write me? . . . "In *The Stork is Dead* you have these forty questions on whether a person is ready for marriage. Don't you think that is a bit much? Couldn't you make it more simple?")

15. "What do you think of nudie movies?" . . . . "How do you feel about the *Playboy* philosophy?" . . . . "Can you tell us what is so terrible about hard-core pornography?"

16. "Why do boys talk about sex all the time?" . . . . "My boy friend has this book showing all the ways to do it. He thinks it is great, but I don't see why" . . . . "I know this nice guy and he is so cool, but everything makes him think of a dirty story. He knows I don't like them, but he tells them anyway. Is he some kind of freak or something?"

17. "Incest" problems: "Should I tell my mother the way my step-father bothers me?" . . . . "I am so afraid. He has told me if I stop him, he might kill me." (Incest is one tough problem. It is also more frequent than the world knows.)

18. The unusuals: Homosexual. . . . Lesbian. . . . Oral intercourse. . . . Anal intercourse. . . . "What's transvestism. . . . sadism. . . . exhibitionism?" . . . . "Our neighbor boy got picked up by the police for window peeping. What is the matter with him?" . . . . "Would you tell me a good definition of a pervert? How can I be sure I am not one?"

19. "Can you get a venereal disease by kissing?" . . . . "I heard that a person can catch syphilis from a toilet. Is that

true?" . . . . "My boy friend says he once had claps. He said it was only fair I should know. Only I hate to let him know how dumb I am. Can you tell me what that is?"

20. The Impotency questions: "Is it true that sex isn't any fun after you are thirty?" . . . . "What I heard is that you better get started because you got only a little time to make it and then you can't do it. Is that on the level?" . . . . "My dad is always talking about how he isn't much good any more" . . . . "Do you mind if I ask whether you are getting any at your age?" . . . . "What is the best age for sex?" (The best eliminator of this confusing misinformation is a wise father.)

These twenty are asked often and in numberless ways. Others of lesser frequency are: "What is the difference between fornication and adultery?" . . . . "I am getting married this summer. Do you think a married couple should tell everything they ever did?" . . . . "How come that boys are so interested in a girl's breasts. There is this nice boy I know but all he wants to do is play around up there. He never tries anything else. I don't understand this" . . . . "I am engaged to a boy who never once tried to do anything more than kiss me. I wonder if this is normal. When I ask him, he tells me he doesn't care about sex. Do you think it will be all right after we are married?" . . . . "What do you do if a girl throws herself at you?" . . . . "I never had a wet dream. Do you think there might be something wrong with me?" . . . . "What do they mean by erogenous zones?" . . . . "How can you tell if a girl is a virgin?" . . . . "What is a climax?" . . . . "What do they mean by 'making out'?" . . . . "Can a nymphomaniac be cured?" . . . . "He gets a strange pleasure from hurting me. Will he get over this?" . . . . "My boy friend says he thinks I am frigid and that there is only one way to find out." ("Lines Guys Use" in *The Stork is Dead* outlines the ingenious approaches boys put to girls for sex. Mothers tell me they are simply variations on an old theme.)

In addition to the heavies there are some from the teeny-boppers, "How can I get him to notice me?" . . . . or, "Her to like me?" . . . . or, "Do you think I have a chance?" First date questions, how to ask. . . . . what to talk about. . . . . when to kiss. . . . . plus many others which seem frivolous maybe, but maybe they're not.

A staggering array of questions, aren't they? But they're all right there in my letter file. To which no parent need panic provided his sons and daughters know the answers. But from what I've seen I must also say—I wouldn't want my children out in society today unless they did!

Twelve

The Parent Alone

Never having been a parent alone, I decided to go to the wellspring. Those faced with this problem would naturally have more to say than I. From the successful parents-alone we have known, I sought advice.

By way of correspondence, phone calls and personal visits, here are the most helpful observations:

"So why make such a big thing of it? Nobody breaks up a home without thinking, do they? I knew it wouldn't be easy. But I was betting I could do as well solo as the two of us botching it together. So I made my choice. Then why should I cry? Sure, it's a tough job. But it wasn't easy the other way either."

"The truth is a lot of the same things apply to one parent the same as they would to two. You just have to try to be twice the person you were before."

"The hardest part for me is to keep from passing on bitterness. I want my children to respect their father for the things that are respectable about him. The fact that he doesn't see it this way, hurts."

"Don't knock daddy. It kicks back at you. The kids' father was terrible. All the snide little things he fed into their heads baffled them. Then it angered them and tended to put up a barrier between them and him."

"I have told my children that they could know anything they want to know about the troubles between me and their mother. But I also made it clear I would never run her down. No child of mine is ever going to be worried about his mother's character because of something I said."

"After my husband died, I played fairies too long. But that's no good. Faith is one thing; pink clouds are something else. You can't beat honesty. You and the kids together better be realistic. Unless you are, they may wind up wondering, 'What's the matter with dear old mom—isn't she very bright?' "

"It seems to me that money problems have a way of getting all out of proportion. Usually you can't afford as much as before. Adjusting is hard. I think the best way to handle this is facing facts together. With mine what they don't know is the most frightening. But there are some good things about it. My children had to get jobs and they are probably learning things this way they never would otherwise."

"Wielding authority alone is my hardest job. I'm a 'patsy' at heart. When we were first divorced, Junior made a monkey out of me. But it wasn't good for him either. So I decided that a firm hand when it's needed gives a child security. Sometimes you have to get hold of yourself and say 'no' and make it stick."

"When there is only one parent, this makes it doubly important that what's left of the family should spend lots of time together."

"As much as possible, eat together; at least one meal a day; it helps to keep you a unit and encourages talk. Actually, we spend more time together now than we did before. So maybe it isn't all bad."

"Don't get all wrapped up in the children with no outside interests. I did for a while and it was a mistake. I made them my whole life. I didn't go anywhere without them, didn't date, always put them first. Suddenly I woke up that I was living their life, not mine. When I decided this was no good, things started to go better. They actually were as tired of me as I was of them. Now I find the more I can relate to other people my own age, the better I can relate to my children."

"My problem is trying to determine just how much I should let my children in on my own hurt. There is this psychologist in our P.T.A. who says you should always keep up a brave front. But I can't help noticing that he is happily married!"

"How do you teach a child with only one parent that love and marriage were meant to be beautiful? Well, it isn't easy. Particularly it isn't, if they are getting a lot of flak from the other side. But some way I've got to do it. What I tell my three, 'Look, I know marriage can be hell. So do you. But I want you to know it can also be good when it's right.' "

"One of my friends said I should let our doctor talk to the boys about sex. But I thought that over and decided no outsider could do this job as well as the one person they needed to trust for everything—me. It wasn't easy but it turned out fine. Now we can talk about anything."

"Maybe you won't like this, but I told my daughters plain that girls without fathers could be an easier make because they want to be close to a man. I didn't grow up yesterday. Men give me the lonesome pitch and it's a cinch my girls will get it too. What I tell them is the old one about 'Keep an open mind, baby, but don't let your brains fall out.' "

"Sewing is a poor substitute for sex in my life. But right now it will have to do. So I make a lot of dresses. Also on the weekend the dog gets walked a lot. I think my children should know that being divorced is lonely. They don't need to know everything, but glossing it all over can't be good either."

"As you know, my children are raised now and, thank the Lord I can be proud of all of them. But if I had it to do over, I would change one thing. We would have spent more for good times instead of saving so hard for the future. I don't mean being wasteful. That's not right. But living when you're together is awfully important too."

"Tell them not to make the mistake I did when my husband died. I had the whole family playing the 'wouldn't-it-be-awful-if' game. Thank goodness before they were all gone, I caught on."

"I think that somehow the parent alone has a special problem when it comes to religion. A child who has lost his father wants to know how we can say God is love. This needs some discussing and an especially loving touch from me."

"If you can manage, it is a good thing to have some family friends who are happily married. For us to be with them now and then seems to do a lot for everybody. It lets us see and feel that marriage can be good. It gives us hope."

(One thing came on strong out of our research here. Martha and I decided we haven't been doing enough for people like this; having them in our home; taking them with us on little trips; just plain loving those whose love isn't as complete as ours. We also decided another thing. We're going to do better.)

Thirteen

Testing! Testing!

It was an important meeting and my signals were "go!" . . . "go!" . . . "go!" I had promised one of the committee chairmen I would meet him early. He had a few minor matters for checking on his report. Most children can sense when parents are "revving" their motors.

Karen could.

She was only four which is a wistful age for us. They need some extra special loving at four.

As I put my hand on the knob, she turned on all her charm. "Daddy," she said in her honey tones, "will you read to me?"

The usual excuses formed on my lips, but something filtered their saying. What came out was, "Sure, sweetie, I'll read to you."

We sat down in our favorite daddy-daughter chair. It was a short book—five chapters.

"How will it be if I read Chapter One tonight and the rest tomorrow?" This she bought. So I read. It couldn't have been more than three minutes. Then I closed the book and said, "Gee, that's an exciting story. I can hardly wait to see how it comes out. Do you think you can stand it till tomorrow?"

"Oh," she answered with all her bells ringing, "I already know. Mommy reads this one to me all the time."

Light on my darkness! How blind can a daddy be!

She didn't want to know what the book said. That she knew by heart. The information she wanted was something else. Did she matter more than a dumb old meeting?

Sure, grownups have things they think are important. But what is more important than a little girl? To which there is only one answer: Nothing!

Large goal sixteen years ago: "I will never say 'no' if I can possibly say 'yes'."

Fourteen

Time to Know Each Other

Most of us operate under the delusion that some day our schedule will open up. Down there in the future we will stumble onto a big chunk of free time. Then we will live it the way it should be.

"Familiar phrases . . . 'When we get the house paid for we can relax'. . . . 'Next month will be less stringent . . . then we can contribute to good causes'. . . . 'The first of the week is a better time to start that diet'. . . . 'If I were to make my reforms on January first, I could more easily measure my progress'. . . . 'When I have a little bit more in the bank, then I will spend time with the wife and family'. . . . Next year! Some day! Tomorrow!" *

These are the echoes of our busy day.

So many problems. So much to do. So how can we find time to keep this pledge to a child, "I promise you that when I am with you, I will really be with you"?

---

* Charlie W. Shedd, *Time for All Things* (Ten Affirmations for the Christian Use of Time) (Nashville: Abingdon Press, 1962).

The answer is, we won't *find* time. We'll have to make it. If this gets done, it will need to be scheduled. And for some of us there is only one way. This is to arrange our affairs with the family in top priority.

Sure, there are seasonal celebrations. Christmas, New Years, Easter, Fourth of July, Thanksgiving. These come on strong for us. Plus all the other specials we can manage, including those wild and woolly locals. "Plum Creek Days" in Nebraska with beards and barbecue. "Cherokee Strip" in Oklahoma. Indians. Horses. Parades. And would you believe "Juneteenth" in Texas?

Rituals for times like this go big with almost everyone. Ask, "What do you remember most about your home?" More often than not the answer centers around holidays, special occasions.

"Well, I'll never forget *Christmas* at our house . . . hiding the presents, and what could we buy for dad because he has everything. Selecting the tree and how crabby we'd get decorating it. I mean always. We'd start out real nice so nobody would get mad. All of a sudden, wham! Somebody would start fighting over the tinsel, or who puts the star on top this year. Candy all over the place—chocolates, peanut brittle, fudge! Mom's wonderful homemade date bread. Remember that beautiful family worship before we opened the presents?"

"*Birthdays,* that's what I remember! We'd pile in the folk's bed early. The sleepy way we'd sing 'Happy Birthday'! All the verses. Grim. But we'd never give up. Then dad would say, 'That's what they must mean by rendering a number.' And the presents. How we could hardly wait for grandma's box 'cause she always sent some little extra for each of us. I'm telling you! Great!"

"What I liked was *Fourth of July*. We had this family picnic, see? Fried chicken, homemade ice cream, the works. All those crazy contests like sack races. With prizes, even. Horseshoes, softball, swimming. Then some more to eat and the fireworks. Every year someone got burned. Never real bad. Wasn't that something?"

"*Vacations*. Did we ever have the vacations! That mountain cabin with fireplace and popcorn . . . The bobcat! Remember the bobcat? . . . And I'll never forget that little old lady in the men's washroom at Santa Fe. Remember what she said and how we all cracked up. But it *was* a dark hall and that sign was kind of battered. Besides, she probably couldn't see well anyway. And Paul said, 'I wonder what she thought the urinal was for.' That really fractured us. Honest, I was afraid we'd die laughing! . . . Our trip to the Capitol and that guide who knocked himself out to entertain us. . . . That cute little house by the seashore, and riding those waves the first time. . . . How our family car seemed to turn in by itself wherever there was a roller coaster. . . . Remember the way Timmy fell in the lake all dressed up ready for church? The money he found at the pier and that reward the man gave him. . . . The way we all got sick in Mexico. . . . How our whole family swam across the Lake of the Ozarks and got our picture in the paper. . . . Those horse games we played in the car and the crazy prizes. . . . That place we went for fried chicken and roasting ears—all you could eat for a dollar! Were they ever glad to see us go! . . . Fabulous, man. Those vacations were simply fabulous. No wonder the folks used to borrow money for vacations."

Fortunate the family with ready recall to these peak experiences. Wise parents will plan and save and float a loan maybe?

And they will know it was worth it, because it makes for healthy memories.

But good as it is, there is a better way. This is to incorporate weekly, monthly, regular celebrations. These can vary. But they must be regular, like *Family night weekly*.

We agree to the day at the first of the week to mesh with everyone's schedule. During the early years we had certain rituals like "romping"; limitless gymnastic techniques. I'll never forget how Karen cried when she finally grew too big. It was during that pudgy girlish period. They were studying prehistoric monsters in science and the timing was bad. "What if I grow that big, Daddy? Could anybody ever love anyone as huge as I am?" (Which they did! And you should see her svelte after two babies!)

Then there were games like "Drop the Handkerchief" and "London Bridge Is Falling Down" which I thought they would never outgrow. Shooting baskets, ping-pong; pool; darts; caroms; checkers—anything with a board; plus our homemade games and a lot of the commercial standbys.

There were "Treasure Hunts" which were strictly our concoction and that has to be good. Stimulating the family to think of their own entertainment may be a lost art. Too bad. Some of our best times came out of pooling our imaginations. There are so many amazing things in the marketplace, we forget an important fact: The things we do on our own have special significance. And they may be the most remembered! Is it because they drew us together in the invention? Whatever the answer, all the family can do together—planning, playing, praying, this has to be good for everyone.

As the children outgrew these, we found an excellent substitute—one night out each week for dinner together. Cost too much? It doesn't need to. What we do is vote and the simple places usually win. Hamburgers and French fries seem to mean as much with the family together as sirloins at the Steak House.

What do we do if it's family night and company comes? It happens very little. This is probably because most of our friends know enough to phone and ask, "Is this the big night at your house?" If it is, they seem to understand with a kind of wistful wishing. Or if we do get stuck, we simply work around it the best we can. After all, sudden adjustment is important too.

Occasionally, we have a family vote on whether to include other people. But that seldom carries. Which says something again about the strong feeling in a child's heart for the family together!

Time alone with dad is our second regular celebration. What this means is that I take each child out for dinner alone monthly. Which is some kind of big deal as you will see from this report: It was a prayer conference in northern Oklahoma. Timothy and I had gone together. The theme was "Family Worship" and I was the speaker. My emphasis was, "Prayer is a good thing, but it isn't enough. Every home needs spiritual unity. But this is more likely to come if there is unity in other places."

Naturally, I discussed our efforts in this direction, but I left out one thing. That night when I tucked Tim in, he reminded me, "Dad, you forgot the neatest part! You didn't tell them how we go out together alone." Which was right. (Timmy usually is.) So I asked him if he'd like to give them the word tomorrow.

You'd have to know this guy to understand that we have here a logical question. He likes to appear in public, even before two hundred people at a prayer conference. On second thought, he does not like it. He loves it! That's how it happened that the next night he gave his testimony. It wrote itself so deeply on me I can recall it word for word:

> My dad forgot to tell you the neatest part. Which is that every month we go out for dinner alone. Then we go to the dime store and buy something I want to buy for fifty cents. Or we go to a show or wherever I want to go. And I wanted to tell you fathers how you should maybe try it some time, because it is real neat!" Long silence; scratching of head; then back to the microphone. "I guess that's all there is to it but it is real neat! You got any questions?" (Normal procedure for these meetings.)

When the applause died down, a little lady from Wichita queried, "Young man, I would like to know what do you and your father discuss at these dinners?"

"Oh," said Tim, like a fast draw on target. "He listens to all my troubles!"

To that, of course, gales of laughter. Which was rather too much for Timothy. "Daddy," he said for everyone's hearing, "I don't think these people think little boys got any troubles!"

But they do!

I wouldn't have any idea how young you go before they don't. But from two up, they do. I know because two is when we started. Which, by the time a child is in college amounts to something like two hundred "one-on-one" sessions together.

Letters to Karen came out of this background. We go back occasionally to the booth at "Ten Fathoms Restaurant" where she said, "Daddy, write me some letters on how to keep

Vincent happy forever!" We also go back to the Oyster House where my oldest son made a similar request. *Letters to Philip* came out of that one.

Do you know what a teddy bear means to a child at four? Or why your six-year-old wants the hall light on when he goes to bed? What's going on up in the tree house at ten-and-a-half? Or the awesome struggle inside your teenager; from *his* viewpoint, do you know?

As I have already said, in our family there is a withdrawal at teen age. Psychiatrists call it "the seclusion syndrome," which has a nice sound. Only we call it "the cave." They make two noises from the cave: "Uh, and Uh, Uh." Which, being interpreted mean "Yes," "No," or "I gotta have the car this Friday!"

Always this is the big question: "How can we bridge the gap?" To which the answer is, "Start when they're two." And if two is long gone, then the time to begin is now. Even in high school, it's not too late.

Sometimes, just for effect, I have said to one of our cave-dwellers, "This is our Saturday out! You rather not go?" Would you believe? Never a single turndown. Why? Is it because they are hoping? Maybe, just maybe, something might turn us on together like back there in our ancient history. And it often does. Real often.

Still it's a difficult question. Why do our children draw the curtain, shut the door, bolt the latch like that? Here is one answer from a teen letter:

> All of a sudden my folks are real buddy-buddy. They keep asking, "Why don't you ever tell us what you're doing? What's going on?" Pushy stuff, like that. Do you know what I think? I think it's a con job. I think they don't trust me and they want to find out some things.

> They must think I'm awful dumb not to catch on.
> Besides what I want to know is where have they been all this time?
> I can remember when I was a kid how I wanted us to be a close family. But it was like they weren't there when I needed them. So, what I'm asking is, why do I need them now?"

Awesome question!

But there is no question about this: The art of parenthood is the art of communication. And communication takes time—time to get your thoughts across—plus more time, much more, to listen to his.

So much listening. You listen and listen and listen. You listen with both ears and you listen with your other one. The one where you hear what they don't say; you listen with that.

You listen to laughter and jokes at their level. You listen to moaning and groaning of things inside.

You listen to noises and chatter and *ad infinitum*. You listen. You talk. You listen some more, talk some more, and you listen more than you talk.

You do this regularly, steady, year after year. And then one day, one great day, you sense a fine thing.

This is no happening. It's a creation. And in all God's creation there are few things created more thrilling than this:

Parent and child—true friends!

Fifteen

Everybody Loved Stephanie

Stephanie was one of the most popular girls I ever knew. Whenever there was an election, the question was, "Who will be elected besides Stephanie."

You wouldn't know it from looking at her. She was really quite plain. Horn-rimmed glasses. Thin.

But everybody loved Stephanie.

One day I asked her, "Steffie, how do you do it?"

"Well," she replied, "I guess it's because I remember something my grandmother taught me. What she said was, 'Never forget, Steffie, everybody is a little bit lonesome.' "

"Could I climb the highest place in Athens, I would lift my voice and proclaim: 'Fellow citizens, why do ye turn and scrape every stone to gather wealth, and take so little care of your children, to whom one day you must relinquish it all?' "

Socrates 469–399 B.C.

The Dignity of Work

"We are not in this world for pleasure,
but to do our damn duty."
Bismarck

One

The Happy Airedale

We once bought a puppy with whom we were given a remarkable lecture. (I know what you're thinking: "which" is correct usage. But most of our dogs have seemed like a "whom.")

The speaker was no ordinary friend of the canine gentry. Under the general theme, "How To Be Worthy of Airedales," he preached for a verdict. Feeding, grooming, handling, showing, training, loving. Provided, of course, you knew about loving Airedales. Which, according to the man, not everybody does.

"You love an Airedale," he said, "with challenge. This is one proud animal. He wants to be useful. And the more you make him feel that way, the better. If he thinks he is not contributing, he will get mean and grouchy and sullen. Then you will both be very unhappy."

This is a parable for parents. In a very real sense children are like Airedales. The more they are trained to feel worthwhile the better.

Question: Who is the most unhappy person on the youth scene today?

Answer: The full-time noncontributor!

"I'm doing my thing," he smirks, "and my thing is to do nothing while others do something so I can do nothing!"

He calls himself "the beautiful people," and he would like us to believe he's arrived. "Here's where it's at," he says. Only it's not where he says it is. And he hasn't arrived nor is he beautiful inside.

You watch him close and you see. His slouch and his sneer are coming through clear. This guy isn't happy. He's miserable. Like the Airedale, non-useful, he's totally wretched.

"So that's how it is, Peter. Life does not owe you a living. There will be days when you wish for a perpetual rest cure. But the bridge to success is never on that side.

"Before the mountains were brought forth, God put things together this way. Happiness is an inside job and work done right is one of its wellsprings. Always for every situation and for everyone, that's how it is.

"Bismarck, the wise old German was right: 'We are not in this world for pleasure, but to do our damn duty!'

"You'd be smart to accept that and make friends with it forever!"

Two

Some "How-To's" on the "Damn Duty"

If work is essential to the child's emotional health, then another parental responsibility comes clear. We must teach our children how to do it effectively. This will require careful planning, lots of discussion and a definite program. As much as possible, it ought to be shaped by all of us together.

There are several work precepts which have become the rule at our house.

1. *Enjoy your work. Some of it, like the man says, is a drudge! So you've got to do it. Your attitude makes all the difference.* Learn the thrill of a challenge. The tougher the assignment, the more fun when you master it. Discipline yourself to do heartily what you do. You can estimate that you will spend one-third of your life at your work. That's too much time to go grumbling. Learning to work with zest is one of the surest sources of mature happiness.

Anyone knows that everything you do, doesn't need full application. Some parts of your job can be done by habit. But otner parts go better at full enthusiasm. Save your "fizz" for these.

2. *We will teach you how to work. If you respond, the whole world will be wanting you.* This is one of the great cries of owners, presidents, supervisors, foremen, all employers—"Where can I get good help?" Always, efficient workers are at a premium. You will be in constant demand if you learn how to do things "decently and in order."

Certain *regular* chores are important to the "work-never-goes away-concept." In our plus mark system there is a definite order of duty. Jobs are alternated for variety and for teaching the "how to."

In addition to these routine responsibilities we have special times of training. Mother at her cooking, sewing, keeping house can begin teaching early. At certain stages children respond well to an opportunity for service. Later there will be a very sharp curve from enthusiasm to total disinterest.

If dad is a gardener, he can educate with seeds and soils and the mysteries of growth. Even mowing the lawn offers an excellent schooling place. Washing the car. Hoeing the weeds. Raking the yard. Painting the fence. All can be valuable "turners-on" of the child's abilities.

Then in addition to these jobs at home, we have another consideration. We must teach our children how to work for other people. There are many ways.

My hobby is woodworking. Each of our five shared some of the shop work with me. Here they learned respect for tools; the danger of sharp things; the beauty of wood; fitting piece to piece; the pride of craftsmanship. In this setting they could also be taught anticipation. The theme was: "Watch me now and see what I'll be needing next. If it's the hammer, have it there ahead of time. Same for the saw and square. When people pay you for working, they are paying you also for thinking. The more you think, the more you are worth."

All of this training can be done in the spirit of fun and great fellowship. And the key to the fun may be in the choices. Example: "We have two jobs to do before dinner. One is to put the tools away. The other is to sweep the shop. Which one would you like to do?"

As I talk with young people I find many lacking in this kind of training. They have a vacuum where their work habits should be. In numberless cases it isn't their fault. No one ever taught them the dignity of work or how to do it.

3. *We expect you to do your fair share. Some jobs are no pay*. Under our plus mark system there are certain unpaid duties. These each member is expected to assume as part of the family. Everyone has his assignment. This begins as early as two and carries on until graduation from high school. Obviously, a three-year-old can't do as much as a Junior Higher. But he can carry out trash, help set the table, and do little errands.

As soon as possible, we get the whole gang on a weekly rotation of specific responsibilities, empty waste baskets and garbage . . . clear the table . . . load the dishwasher . . . feed the pets.

We have had many pets including the customary dogs and cats, plus birds, fish, rodents and however you classify turtles. Then there were five horses. The happiest day in a child's life is when he buys his horse. His next happiest day is when he sells it. (Horses always sell for half what they cost. But the relief in labor more than makes up the depreciation.) The reason for this parade of mares and geldings is our family rule on horses. It is well understood before the purchase. And the rule is: whenever mom and dad start shoveling manure, the horse has to go.

All of our pets of every specie have added much to our family living. Perhaps their greatest contribution has been training in work habits. Feeding and care of live animals, along with the loving involved, is a great educator.

The philosophy behind our plus mark system is two-fold: (1) "You are entitled to a certain amount each week as your share in the family income; (2) You are responsible for certain services without pay as your share of the family work."

In addition to the rotating jobs, each child is to care for his own room. He is expected to make his bed daily. Other than this, his room is his own castle or his pigsty. Some children are neat by nature. Others prefer to live where it looks like a twister has just passed through. Strange how two in the same family can be so totally different. Interesting too how one child can vary so much from stage to stage. We find it best to say, "Our only room-rule is: make your bed every day; don't write on the walls; and if it gets too bad, we'll keep your door closed."

Wise parents know this for a fact: the less we harrass our child at any point, the better our communication later. Part of the generation gap at the teen level is traceable to things past. Sometimes we made molehills into mountains. Any contention which can be eliminated, should be. Room service is one of these.

So also is the grade business. Some parents make a big thing of paying for school marks. We don't. For us, another place where the point applies—"We expect you to do your best."

We do help our children with homework. Provided it's legal. We pitch right in. How do we know if it's legal? We ask our children to ask their teachers. Then we take their word for it. Most teachers say they wish parents would show more interest. Studying with each other, working on assignments, drawing, building, outlining—these all offer added opportunity for communication.

Any policy which avoids arguments before we get to them has to be good. How the room looks; what's on that grade card; how much should we help with the school work—these can be decided well in advance for the avoidance of conflict.

Another question for pre-settling is, "What extra work earns extra money?" Our practice is that we pay for jobs we would have to hire done. Mowing the lawn; washing the car; baby-sitting.

If there is a question about rate of pay; whether the job qualifies for extra money; is someone being treated unjustly?; we vote. As in every other situation, majority rule brings us closer together. It also leaves that all-important feeling of fairness.

4. *The world admires ingenuity. Be inventive.* We will show you what to do. At first we will even show you how to do it. Then you put your head to it and do it your way. Experiment.

Usually the main thing is to get going when you have something to do. Some wag has said, "I like work. It fascinates me. I can sit and look at it for hours." So can most of us. But you do yourself a big favor when you learn the art of a quick takeoff. Sometimes you will do the hard part first so the easy stuff seems easier. Other times you'll begin light and work up to the tough things. Which way you do on a certain day may depend on your mood. Learn to measure yourself and your energy against the job and its challenge.

All of which is to say once more—*think!* Some jobs require all muscle and little brains. For others the difference is head-work. Planning ahead can save you time and make it more fun.

5. *Learn the art of doing nothing well. Leisure is important to work. Relaxing, resting, sleeping, playing, are all part*

of an intelligent life. Your daily quiet time, annual vacations together, each simple little goof-off can serve you well. The wise person develops a rhythm. It is a rhythm with purpose. We retreat to restore body and soul. We go forward for service.

Teaching a child to relax is one of our responsibilities. We make a mistake when we say, "Don't just sit there—do something." The result of unnecessary drive-drive-drive can be sick perfectionism.

Some leisure time might well be given to care of the body. This may require no guidance. If the child is interested in sports he could get all the exercise he needs as a result of that tendency. Fathers who make a big thing of athletics (or wished they had) might need to guard against being pushy in this direction. But in the best way possible we should be sure our children get this message:

> Take care of your body. It's the only one you'll ever have. Without being a nut on physical fitness, you would do well to use some of your leisure for exercise. You can do better work and it will be more enjoyable if you feel well.

Three

Giving and Saving and a Good Time Spending

From my more heated teen letters comes this burner:

> Every time I put the bite on my old man, I get the same bull. "Who do you think you are, the last of the big spenders? Didn't I just give you five? What you doing anyway? Playing the horses or something? Blah! Blah! Blah!" My mom says he's only kidding. Well, I'm not. I don't know how much more I can take. And you know what burns me most? He's being so darn stupid!

It is difficult for adults to understand the economic distress of these characters. For years the teenager has been presenting his wants (sometimes his needs) before the parental court. He's won some, lost some. Every mom and dad knows he's won more than he's lost. But he doesn't know it. In his mind this is a losing business and the whole thing is beginning to drag. Will this kind of scrounging never end?

Which looks like gross exaggeration to us. But not to him. Exaggeration, the two hundred percent kind is one of his specialities. And so is another meanie which dovetails now with that one—ingratitude!

As parents, it is easy for us to operate under this delusion—the more we give the more they will love us. With which conclusion there is only one thing wrong. It is not that way. In their teen years the reverse is true. As the cash passes, there may be a twinge of "I guess they're okay." But the long-range emotion is another thing—humiliation!

Any effective program for allowances, payments, and money management remembers these things. The more we protect the teenager's dignity; the more we recognize his fierce sense of pride; the more we remove unnecessary financial irritants; the better our chances for gratitude via compliments.

In our program for "full-management-by-your-Junior-year," there is an interesting turn of events. The gratitude thing takes care of itself. Regularly, our children are getting the "lucky you" treatment from their peers.

"Wow! You mean they give you all that dough?"

"Did you hear that? He gets a car with his driver's license!"

"Boy, would I like to have what you got!"

"Wish I had folks like yours!"

It is not that our children tell us what their friends say. Nor is it that their friends tell us. But their friends telling them gets the job done. After all, at this age there is no higher authority than someone this age.

Where we get clued in is from parents who call. "What's going on over there? . . . That's all we're hearing over here . . . Is it a fact that?" . . . (any one of numberless reports, some true, some distorted, some funny). But however they come, we know one thing for sure. Money matters are more enjoyable here because of this feed back.

Threats from Outside and Inside

They are also being told another thing. This comes in several versions, which when put together means: "You'd be a fool to blow a deal like that!"

Generally speaking, threats are ineffective. Unless, of course, they come from those brilliant teenagers around them. Whereupon they are worth considering.

"Gee your folks sure must think a lot of you," does two things. It makes the child feel good about himself. It also racks up Brownie points for mom and dad. Plus, it very likely does a third thing. After it has settled in the soul it comes back like this—"You *really would* be a fool if you blew it."

Working for Other People

After we have trained our children in the "how to's," they generally do better elsewhere. Our policy is to open up any door we can, provided the child wants our help. He usually does at first. Later he may prefer to get his own jobs. This tends to test his ingenuity and bring him a special sense of satisfaction.

We know a boy, who during his sophomore year in high school, studied diesel motors as a sideline. The next summer he hired himself out to a contractor as a diesel mechanic's helper. During a year when summer jobs were scarce, he was snapped up immediately at a high hourly rate.

We know another boy who, during his junior year in college, took a computer key punch course. The next semester he got a job with the Internal Revenue Service. Working four hours a day, at above average earnings, he helped pay for his education. In addition he had those satisfactions which can only come from ingenuity sparked by independence.

We know a teenage girl who developed gift-wrapping to an art. During Christmas and other holidays she was much in demand. Several stores welcomed her services for the added touch she could put to a package.

Money earned outside the home can be adjusted to the regular monthly allowance. Some students need full time at their studies. Others do better the more they have to do.

During summer vacations our plus marks and allowances are discontinued for the older children. The theme for these three months is, "Scrabble. Earn your own money."

We go 50-50 on items which are best handled together. As previously explained, this is true on the first automobile. The same goes for other major purchases. What's a major purchase? If there is any question, we vote. Things like a horse, new bicycle, ham radio equipment call for partnership. Any place where child and adult work together is good for growing communication.

How Much Should Children Know About Family Finances?

Rule for our family: Things go better when everyone has the total financial picture. Even the young child can better understand his allowance when set against all other expenditures. Church, savings, insurance, utilities, home repairs are likely to come as a surprise to him. He knows about food and clothing, but it is well for him to know about other necessities.

He should also have a bit of training on these—investments and interest, stocks and bonds, deposits and withdrawals. At the right time he should be shown how to write a check and how to balance accounts.

Having educated him, we do well to leave plenty of room for self-management. Policy worth considering: "We want you to know anything you want to know about our finances. We only want to know what you want us to know about yours."

The Secret Is at the Outlet.

Our underlying theme continues to be: Give ten percent. Save ten percent. Spend the rest with thanksgiving and praise.

This is our slogan and we have taught it to our children from infancy up.

Early and with clear voice they hear us say:

> You can never outgive God. At the heart of the universe there is a law that love comes back to the lover. Blessings return to the blesser. Gifts circle back to the giver. So, when you run into trouble take your eyes off the intake. Concentrate on the outlets. You do not give in order to get. That's phoney and God knows a phoney every time. But when you do give abundantly, you will receive abundantly. So watch the first ten percent to be sure you're giving enough away. Watch the next ten percent to be sure you're putting enough away. You will have more fun with the eighty percent if you keep the first twenty channeled right.

Four

Paul, in Praise of Work!

This book has been a family project. We had several wild and woolly sessions putting it together. The first of these was a week's vacation in the Virgin Islands. Ten of us met—two parents, five offspring, two in-laws, one grandchild—for fun and a foundation group-think. References and quotations have been checked at later meetings. There have been numerous phone calls, letters, and personal visits. Each individual has had opportunity to approve the final manuscript.

Here is an excerpt from one of Paul's letters as he muses on work and money. At this writing he is a senior at an American university. In addition to his studies, he is employed four hours daily in an interesting position. This explains his reference to "the pleasure I still get from being responsible to my part-time job."

"The sense of satisfaction I now get from having a job while I'm in school must be traceable to the days when I worked for plus marks. That system was a great invention for giving us kids a sense of economic reality. First, I learned that money and the things it buys weren't all mine for the asking. I had to work for and save nickels for the neat doodads I had to have and for what I wanted to do. And that, of course, made them all the more valuable to me.

"I can remember the gratifying feeling of accomplishment—along with stiff muscles or hammered thumbs—from seeing the freshness of a lawn I'd just mowed or the progress on some project I'd helped with in your woodshop. It's akin to the pleasure I still get from being responsible to my part-time job, even though there are times when I'd rather be doing other things.

"Even more important, I think, by encouraging me to work, you ingrained in me a feeling for the dignity of work in and of itself."

Five

The Joy Is in Deserving

Talmadge was one fine boy.

He came from a second rate background. Not that he was neglected in the customary sense. But all the inferior parent-child relationships are not in poverty situations. There are pockets of luxury, too, where children are deprived.

That's how it was with Talmadge. His folks had everything, including nothing to live for. So they partied, drank too much, and had little time for their only son.

To make it up they lavished him with things. Things he wanted and things he didn't—they poured it on. On him, on themselves, they spent money like it was going out of style. Which it probably never would for them. They had that kind of holdings.

Yet Talmadge was one of those "in-spite-of-his-background" people. Something strong inside him seemed to defy all the rules of reaction. Like the old motto says, "Same fire hardens the egg and melts the butter."

That's how it was with Talmadge. He seemed to harden at the right places and soften where he should. All the time he kept coming on stronger. He grew more mellow while he grew more determined.

He had a big smile, the kind which starts way down and draws the circle larger. Talmadge loved everyone and everyone loved him; and I did.

How I knew about his shattering experience was that he told me. I also learned from him something I needed. It is this hard truth for parents: *Sometimes the loving thing is to keep hands off!*

I've always had trouble with that one. There is this thing in me which tends to overprotect. When my children hurt, I hurt and I don't like it. When they succeed I thrill and I do like that. This is how it is and I'm sorry it's always been there in overabundance.

I remember the way Philip put it. He was drawing a picture one day and struggling. It didn't look like a pony and the prospects were not promising. So I drew him a pony. Spots. Long mane. Bridle. Saddle. Nice pony. Which he studied awhile, then said, "But Daddy, I wanted a pony *I* drew."

Most parents will get it. This over-doing is one of our temptations in love. We tend to forget—life isn't all winning for anyone! If there would never be disappointments; if every day his sun shone; that would be one thing. But since it won't, I better not try to push it into that mold.

To forget this can damage way down inside. That's what happened to Talmadge.

He was attending a military academy in our town. It was a fashionable school, one of the best in the Southwest. The reason he was there wasn't good. But he was making the best of it.

His parents had gone off again. This time on a world tour with the jet set. They would be gone several months so that's how he came our way.

He really did like it though. He liked the discipline. He liked the guys. He liked the horses. He liked the golf course and the country club lake for fishing. Plus, he especially liked the photography lab.

He also liked our church youth group. Which I am glad he did, because that's how we came to be close friends. It is also how I got in on this unusual plan he developed.

All his life, he said, he wanted to *earn* something. Which sounds strange to most of us. But it certainly didn't to Talmadge. Just once he wished he could do something his folks couldn't help him with.

You will recognize here that his was some kind of special maturity. For a boy of fourteen, I thought it bordered on greatness. What he decided was that he would buy a camera.

So he picked out this extra high-powered, super-fine Rolleflex. Here it was on page thirty-seven. See? And he opened the catalog to spread it reverently before me. How did I like it and wasn't it beautiful?

It was. Even I, who knew nothing about these things, could see it was beautiful. But the really beautiful part was how he intended to get it.

He would *work* for it. He would hire himself out for odd jobs and earn it. He would save and sweat and do it the hard way. He would put the picture up in his room. He would look at it and dream. Then under his dreams he would build a foundation and "Oh boy . . . won't it be something?"

He began by working for the stable master. Cleaning stalls, currying horses, pitching hay. He also mowed the Adjutant's yard, swept the cafeteria, and worked in the kitchen cleanup.

All of which, you see, took some kind of special courage. It would have been so easy to get it the easy way. But this was Talmadge's deal with Talmadge. It was his own personal, well-thought-out, privately-drawn-up declaration of independence. In his head and his heart a very fine sound. Like the ring of the liberty bell. Loud. Good.

Where he made his mistake, he said looking back, was because of the school paper. One week there was this story about him and he got carried away. It was natural they should take notice. This would be news in a setting like that. Crazy, man! "Poor little rich kid goes to work." Naturally they wouldn't say it that way, but it was news. So the student reporter put it in his "Have you Heard?" column.

Talmadge didn't mind. He liked it. In fact, he liked it so much he decided to send it to his mom and dad. Halfway around the world he sent the clipping.

Maybe you'll think he should have thought that through. And you're right. But he was only fourteen. At fourteen you haven't quit hoping. So he hoped his folks would like the story. He also hoped another thing. Would they maybe be proud? Would they be saying, "Hey, look at the kid! Read this! Earning his own Rolleflex! How do you like that?" Do you suppose they'd understand?

Which I regret to report, they did not.

Oh, sure, they read it. They also got very excited. Only, in their alcoholic fog the real message didn't come through. What did was something else. They saw their dear little Talmadge struggling and they would come to the rescue.

It was Easter weekend. Most of the boys were gone for the holiday. But Talmadge decided to stay. With the cadets away, there were so many extra-money jobs around the academy. Some of them paid time and a half. Which meant he could sock it away all week and make his purchase sooner.

He'd been saving three months and it looked now like late April. This way he might push that up two weeks or three.

Then came Good Friday and always that day I think of Talmadge. I see him sitting there telling his pastor, bleeding inside. And my heart hurts when I remember.

First there was the phone call. Of all the crazy things! His parents had this wild idea, see? They would surprise him. Big deal! They'd come early. What's a little trip from Bimini for a major event like this? And the major event was—I honestly hate to tell you.

They brought him his Rolleflex! I remember the way he described it and I loved how hard he was trying. He wanted to see it their way. Which isn't exactly easy when they arrived like they did—too much in their cups—too much of a giddy blather —"Here it is, kid! We bought it for a surprise, see? Don't mention it! Glad to do it! Hope you enjoy it!"

Like I said, he wanted to see it their way. The minute they got his clipping they had this big idea. They would get in touch with their agent and he would call in the order. Then it would be there waiting when they arrived in the States. If they made connections, if everything swung together, they could be there Easter weekend. That would beat him to it. He couldn't possibly have it by Easter. "And that will be some kind of kicks, right? . . . . Beautiful! . . . . But that's what families are for! Right? . . . . They're for letting them know you care, aren't they? . . . . So there's nothing too good for the kid. Right? . . . . No sir, nothing too good for the kid!"

There are some things so vivid you better not try to describe them. So we'll bring the curtain down here.

Only I thought you would like to know one thing. It was something he said. Sorry I can't give you his inflections. But you will sense that unusual maturity again.

Right here in the middle of his mixed emotions—love, pity, hate, and shadings in blue confusion—all at once he said this thing. It is one of the great statements I've heard from a suffering teenager: "When I get a boy," he said, "I'm going to try and remember. Kids want to do some things themselves. *Besides I think you can't really have fun with something unless you know you deserve it.*"

Six

Hell Raisers for Heaven's Sake

"This year why don't you raise more hell and fewer dahlias."

That's what the man said to the Garden Clubs, and it comes on strong. Most of us delight in this sort of thing, but not for long maybe.

When we run it by a few times, the emphasis changes. It comes on different now with questions. Penetrating questions like, "Do *you* give too much time to trivia?"

To which there is only one answer, with one conclusion. And the conclusion is that somebody raising hell sometimes is a very good thing.

Which makes me wonder about all those ugly shouts of the angry young these days. What effect are they having really? If we could sit on a cloud in time, how would we see it?

Could it be good? I for one think it could be and is!

Some of them are worse than we were. That's for sure. But more of them are better, much better. They have a greater concern, far greater. They recognize the phoney like we never did. They refuse to sit still for some things we took as part of the landscape.

Racial inequality; the futility of war; the injustice of poverty; pollution and the earth's desecration—we really have done one sorry job with these things, haven't we?

Can we deny it?

Too many of us have prettied our gardens while the garbage stacked high elsewhere.

That being the case, the fury of the young could indicate progress. It might even mean that they are greater than we were at their age.

Yet, are they great enough? Frankly, I don't think so. The more I feel their heat up close, the more I doubt their greatness. And I question their hell-raising ability at two points: Some don't know for sure what they are raising hell about; too many who do know are not doing it intelligently!

I don't believe this generation will get the job done. I think their major contribution has been focusing our attention on the evils of society.

What we need now is a set of future citizens concentrating on the cure. Which leads us back down the road again to the home.

Some of us have never thought of it like this. Shouldn't the family curriculum include some courses in "How To Stir Up a Fuss In The Right Way At The Right Time About The Right Things"?

I think it should! And that is one more reason for this book.

On the dumps of history bleach the bones of countless people who didn't have it. What they didn't have was the ability to see their evils and correct them.

So this is my prayer for Peter and all the sons and daughters of men:

> "Lord, I want to remember that my children are not my children. Let me let them manage themselves at the

right pace. May they have the self-respect which comes from a growing self-government. Free them from unnecessary resentment that they may think cool.

"From infancy up, may they know how to love because they have seen love at its best. Here in our home may they be taught that they are children of God. And may they sense the Divine in others also.

"May they know the joy of work well done. Early may they learn what they need for discipline and staying power. As they tie in to the problems of society, may they be angry when they should as they should."

"For the future of all, this is my prayer—*that they may be intelligent hell-raisers for heaven's sake!"*

gives straight answers to teens' honest questions. In language teenagers can accept and trust.

- THE FAT IS IN YOUR HEAD. Dynamic support for the dieter. Helps you accept the fact that you're overweight, overindulging, and doomed to lose the battle, not the bulge, if you're secretly drooling at the anticipation of diet's end. Helps you find the cure in your soul by developing a lifestyle that makes thinness an inspired state of mind. (Cassette package available including book and tape. Features Dr. Shedd with meditations for each day of the month.)

- THE EXCITING CHURCH series. Dr. Shedd studies exciting, attracting, thriving churches to discover the keys to their vitality. Each book offers insights and suggestions for putting one key factor to use in your own church.

- THE EXCITING CHURCH: WHERE PEOPLE REALLY PRAY. Special emphasis on the concept of prayer as first opening up to God rather than trying to get through to Him. Includes a practical plan for leading church members into a workable prayer partnership.

- THE EXCITING CHURCH: WHERE THEY REALLY USE THE BIBLE. Tells of the amazing energy resource we have in total, outspoken reliance on the Bible—in the pulpit, classes, study groups. Offers a helpful checklist for keeping preaching biblically relevant, patterns for going through the Scriptures, practical guidelines for personal study.

THE EXCITING CHURCH: WHERE THEY GIVE THEIR MONEY AWAY. Shows how to get local congregations so turned on they can stop moaning about budgets and bills. Based on the biblical principle that God will provide plenty of income when the outgo meets his approval. Includes proven suggestions to increase church giving, alternatives to gimmicks nobody likes, unusual plans for fund-raising campaigns.